John Home

Douglas

A Tragedy

John Home

Douglas
A Tragedy

ISBN/EAN: 9783744661584

Printed in Europe, USA, Canada, Australia, Japan

Cover: Foto ©Thomas Meinert / pixelio.de

More available books at **www.hansebooks.com**

DOUGLAS;

A

TRAGEDY.

BY JOHN HOME.

As performed at the Theatres Royal of

LONDON AND EDINBURGH.

NON EGO SUM VATES, SED PRISCI CONSCIUS ÆVI.

Had some good angel op'd to me the Book
Of Providence, and let me read my life;
My heart had broke, when I beheld the sum
Of ills, which one by one I have endur'd.
—But God, whose ministers good angels are,
Hath shut the book, in mercy to mankind.

EDINBURGH:

Printed for JOHN BEUGO, ENGRAVER, *and sold by*
ALL THE BOOKSELLERS.

Anno 1792.

DOUGLAS.

The circumstances which attended the publication of this Tragedy mark so strongly the character of the age, and of the country in which it appeared, that they ought never to be forgotten. It was represented in the Edinburgh Theatre, at the close of the year 1756, under the management of Mr. Digges, who himself performed the part of Douglas. The orthodox, both clergy and laity, in that city, and throughout all Scotland, were instantly alarmed. It appeared to them a strange, and almost unaccountable phoenomenon, that a minister of their church should have been guilty of the *crying sin* of writing one of the most beautiful dramatic performances in the English language. Inflammatory pamphlets, advertisements, and handbills appeared. The presbytery of Edinburgh denounced seven clergymen, who had been present at the exhibition of the tragedy, to the several presbyteries in which they resided. These gentlemen confessed the criminality of their own conduct, submitted with humility to the censures of the church, and were forgiven. One of them, a member of the presbytery of Edinburgh, was suspended for some time, with every mark of disgrace, from the exercise of his ecclesiastical functions, although he pleaded in alleviation of the charge,---" that
" he had gone to the play-house only once, and en-
" deavoured to conceal himself in a corner, to avoid
" giving offence; expressing his deep sorrow for what
" he had done, and firm resolution to be more cir-

"cumspect for the future." Another of these gentlemen, Dr. Carlisle, a friend of the Author, who ventured to attempt only a partial and faint vindication of himself, was prosecuted in full form. The Articles of the Libel against him were three---his having gone into the company of Players---his directing them during the rehearsal-- and, lastly, his having been present at the representation of a tragedy, which, in the opinion of the Reverend Divines of those days, contains dreadful oaths and mock prayers, and encourages suicide. The cause went thro' all the courts up to the General Assembly, and Dr. Carlisle every where met with censure and rebuke from his incensed brethren.

In the mean time, the Arch-offender, the accomplished Author of all this scandal to the pious, was commanded to appear before his presbytery at Haddington, on the 5th April 1757. He obtained a delay to the 1st of May thereafter, and during this interval his tragedy was presented with great applause at London in Covent-garden Theatre. Finding it impossible to soften the stern spirit of the Presbyterian Church, he thought proper, in order to avoid a formal degradation from his office, to preach to his congregation at Athelstonford, his farewell sermon, which is said to have drawn tears from the eyes of the people; and two days thereafter, he resigned his charge to his presbytery at Haddington.

Notwithstanding all this, however, when we regard Mr. HOME as holding a place among the list of British Poets, his destiny has been fortunate and happy. A pension from the Crown, which he obtained by means of the late E. of Bute, and the place of Scots Conservator at Campvere, which he was permitted to dispose of to advantage, amply consoled him for the loss of the very moderate emoluments of a Scotch minister. He has also enjoyed a singular piece of felicity, which falls to the lot of few. He has not only seen his reputation flourish in his own days, but he has even lived to see the narrow prejudices of his country pass away. The Clergy of the Church of Scotland, who once persecuted Mr. Home, now regard it as one of the highest honours of their order, to have numbered among its members the Author of the Tragedy of Douglas.

It may perhaps be proper to add, as a curious fact, that notwithstanding the great interest of the Author, Mr. Garrick refused to bring forward this tragedy at Drury-lane as too simple and undramatic. But this celebrated performer had the mortification to see it immediately introduced at Covent-garden with the greatest success; a success that seems rather to increase than to diminish by the course of years.

F.

PROLOGUE
SPOKEN BY MR. SPARKS.

IN ancient times, when Britain's trade was arms,
And the lov'd music of her youth, alarms;
A god-like race sustain'd fair England's fame:
Who has not heard of gallant Piercy's name?
Ay, and of Douglas? Such illustrious foes
In rival Rome and Carthage never rose!
From age to age bright shone the British fire,
And every hero was a hero's sire.
When powerful fate decreed one warrior's doom,
Up sprung the phoenix from his father's tomb.
But whilst those generous rivals fought and fell,
Those generous rivals lov'd each other well:
Tho' many a bloody field was lost and won,
Nothing in hate, in honour all was done.
When Piercy wrong'd, defy'd his prince or peers,
Fast came the Douglas with the Scottish spears;
And, when proud Douglas made his King his foe,
For Douglas, Piercy bent his English bow.
Expell'd their native homes by adverse fate,
They knock'd alternate at each other's gate:
Then blaz'd the castle, at the midnight hour,
For him whose arms had shook its firmest tower.

 This night a Douglas your protection claims;
A wife! a mother! pity's softest names:
The story of her woes indulgent hear,
And grant your suppliant all she begs, a tear:
In confidence she begs, and hopes to find
Each English breast, like noble Piercy's, kind.

PROLOGUE
SPOKEN AT EDINBURGH.

IN days of classic fame, when Persia's Lord
Oppos'd his millions to the Grecian sword,
Flourish'd the state of Athens, small her store,
Rugged her soil, and rocky was her shore,
Like Caledonia's: yet she gain'd a name
That stands unrivall'd in the rolls of fame.

  Such proud pre-eminence not valour gave,
(For who than Sparta's dauntless sons more brave?)
But learning, and the love of every art,
That virgin Pallas and the muse impart.

  Above the rest the Tragic Muse admir'd
Each Attic breast with noblest passion fir'd.
In peace their poets with their heroes shar'd
Glory, the hero's and the bard's reward.
The Tragic Muse each glorious record kept,
And, o'er the kings she conquer'd, Athens wept ‖.

  Here let me cease, impatient for the scene,
To you I need not praise the Tragic Queeen:
Oft has this audience soft compassion shown
To woes of heroes, heroes not their own.
This night our scenes no common tear demand,
He comes, the hero of your native land!
DOUGLAS, a name through all the world renown'd,
A name that rouses like the trumpet's sound!
Oft have your fathers, prodigal of life,
A Douglas follow'd through the bloody strife;
Hosts have been known at that dread name to yield,
And, Douglas dead, his name hath won the field.

‖ *See the* Persai *of Aeschylus.*

Listen attentive to the various tale,
Mark if the author's kindred feelings fail;
Sway'd by alternate hopes, alternate fears,
He waits the test of your congenial tears.
If they shall flow, back to the Muse he flies,
And bids your heroes in succession rise;
Collects the wand'ring warriors as they roam,
Douglas assures them of a welcome home.

DRAMATIS PERSONAE.

	Drury-lane.	Covent-Garden.	Edinburgh.
MEN.			
LORD RANDOLPH,	Mr. Aicken.	Mr. Farren.	Mr. Bell.
GLENALVON,	Mr. Palmer.	Mr. Harley.	Mr. Woods.
NORVAL,	Mr. Bensley.	Mr. Aicken.	Mr. S. Kemble.
DOUGLAS,	Mr. Kemble.	Mr. Holman.	Mr. Kemble.
WOMEN.			
LADY RANDOLPH,	Mrs. Siddons.	Mrs. Pope.	Mrs. Siddons.
ANNA,	Mrs. Ward.	Mrs. Rock.	Mrs. Woods.

' *The passages omitted in representation are marked by inverted commas.*'

DOUGLAS.

ACT I.

SCENE---*The Court of a Castle surrounded with Woods.*

Enter LADY RANDOLPH.

YE woods and wilds, whose melancholy gloom
Accords with my soul's sadness, and draws forth
The voice of sorrow from my bursting heart,
Farewell a while: I will not leave you long;
For in your shades I deem some spirit dwells,
Who from the chiding stream, or groaning oak,
Still hears and answers to Matilda's moan.
O Douglas! Douglas! if departed ghosts
Are e'er permitted to review this world,
Within the circle of that wood thou art,
And with the passion of immortals hear'st
My lamentation: hear'st thy wretched wife
Weep for her husband slain, her infant lost.
My brother's timeless death I seem to mourn,
Who perish'd with thee on this fatal day:
To thee I lift my voice; to thee address
The plaint which mortal ear has never heard.
O disregard me not; though I am call'd
Another's now, my heart is wholly thine.
Incapable of change, affection lies
Buried, my Douglas, in thy bloody grave.

But Randolph comes, whom fate has made my Lord,
To chide my anguish, and defraud the dead.

Enter RANDOLPH.

RAN. Again these weeds of woe! say, do'st thou well
To feed a passion which consumes thy life?
The living claim some duty; vainly thou
Bestow'st thy cares upon the silent dead.

LADY RAN. Silent, alas! is he for whom I mourn:
Childless, without memorial of his name,
He only now in my remembrance lives.
' This fatal day stirs my time-settled sorrow,
' Troubles afresh the fountain of my heart.

' RAN. When was it pure of sadness! These black weeds
' Express the wonted colour of thy mind,
' For ever dark and dismal. Seven long years
' Are pass'd, since we were join'd by sacred ties:
' Clouds all the while have hung upon thy brow,
' Nor broke, nor parted by one gleam of joy.
' Time, that wears out the trace of deepest anguish,
' As the sea smooths the prints made in the sand,
' Has past o'er thee in vain.

' LADY RAN. If time to come
' Should prove as ineffectual, yet, my Lord,
' Thou canst not blame me. When our Scottish youth
' Vy'd with each other for my luckless love,
' Oft I besought them, I implor'd them all
' Not to assail me with my father's aid,
' Nor blend their better destiny with mine.
' For melancholy had congeal'd my blood,
' And froze affection in my chilly breast.
' At last my Sire, rous'd with the base attempt
' To force me from him, which thou rend'redst vain,
' To his own daughter bow'd his hoary head,
' Besought me to commiserate his age,

' And vow'd he should not, could not die in peace,
' Unless he saw me wedded, and secur'd
' From violence and outrage.   Then, my Lord!
' In my extreme distress I call'd on thee,
' Thee I bespake, profess'd my strong desire
' To lead a single, solitary life,
' And begg'd thy nobleness not to demand
' Her for a wife whose heart was dead to love.
' How thou persisted'st after this, thou know'st,
' And must confess that I am not unjust,
' Nor more to thee than to myself injurious.

  ' RAN. That I confess ; yet ever must regret
' The grief I cannot cure.   Would thou wert not
' Compos'd of grief and tenderness alone,
' But had'st a spark of other passions in thee,
' Pride, anger, vanity, the strong desire
' Of admiration, dear to woman-kind ;
' These might contend with, and allay thy grief,
' As meeting tides and currents smooth our frith.

  ' LADY RAN. To such a cause the human mind oft owes
' Its transient calm, a calm I envy not.

  RAN. Sure thou art not the daughter of Sir Malcolm :
Strong was his rage, eternal his resentment :
For when thy brother fell, he smil'd to hear
That Douglas' son in the same field was slain.

  LADY RAN. Oh! rake not up the ashes of my fathers:
Implacable resentment was their crime,
And grievous has the expiation been.
Contending with the Douglas, gallant lives
Of either house were lost ; my ancestors
Compell'd, at last, to leave their ancient seat
On Tiviot's pleasant banks ; and now, of them
No heir is left.   Had they not been so stern,
I had not been the last of all my race.

RAN. Thy grief wrests to its purposes my words.
I never ask'd of thee that ardent love
Which in the breasts of fancy's children burns.
Decent affection and complacent kindness
Were all I wish'd for ; but I wish'd in vain.
Hence with the less regret my eyes behold
The storm of war that gathers o'er this land :
If I should perish by the Danish sword,
Matilda would not shed one tear the more.

LADY RAN. Thou do'st not think so : woeful as I am,
I love thy merit, and esteem thy virtues.
But whither goest thou now?

RAN. Straight to the camp,
Where every warrior on the tip-toe stands
Of expectation, and impatient asks
Each who arrives, if he is come to tell,
The Danes are landed.

LADY RAN.   O, may adverse winds,
Far from the coast of Scotland, drive their fleet !
And every soldier of both hosts return
In peace and safety to his pleasant home !

RAN. Thou speak'st a woman's, hear a warrior's
    wish :
Right from their native land, the stormy north,
May the wind blow, till every keel is fix'd
Immoveable in Caledonia's strand !
Then shall our foes repent their bold invasion,
And roving armies shun the fatal shore.

' LADY RAN. War I detest ; but war with foreign foes,
' Whose manners, language, and whose looks are strange,
' Is not so horrid, nor to me so hateful,
' As that which with our neighbours oft we wage.
' A river here, there an ideal line
' By fancy drawn, divides the sister kingdoms.
' On each side dwells a people similar,

‘ As twins are to each other ; valiant both ;
‘ Both for their valour famous thro' the world.
‘ Yet will they not unite their kindred arms,
‘ And, if they must have war, wage distant war,
‘ But with each other fight in cruel conflict.
‘ Gallant in strife, and noble in their ire,
‘ The battle is their pastime. They go forth
‘ Gay in the morning, as to summer sport ;
‘ When ev'ning comes, the glory of the morn,
‘ The youthful warrior is a clod of clay.
‘ Thus fall the prime of either hapless land :
‘ And such the fruit of Scots and English wars.
 ‘ RAN. I'll hear no more : this melody would make
‘ A soldier drop his sword, and doff his arms,
‘ Sit down and weep the conquests he has made ;
‘ Yea, (like a monk,) sing rest and peace in heav'n
‘ To souls of warriors in his battle slain.'
Lady, farewell : I leave thee not alone;
Yonder comes one whose love makes duty light. [*Exit.*

Enter ANNA.

 ANN. Forgive the rashness of your Anna's love :
Urg'd by affection, I have thus presum'd
To interrupt your solitary thoughts ;
And warn you of the hours that you neglect,
And lose in sadness.
 LADY RAN.   So to lose my hours
Is all the use I wish to make of time.
 ANN. To blame thee, Lady, suits not with my state :
But sure I am, since death first prey'd on man,
Never did sister thus a brother mourn.
What had your sorrows been if you had lost,
In early youth, the husband of your heart ?
 LADY RAN. Oh !
 ANN. Have I distress'd you with officious love,
And ill-tim'd mention of your brother's fate ?

B

Forgive me, Lady : humble tho' I am,
The mind I bear partakes not of my fortune :
So fervently I love you,,that to dry
These piteous tears, I'd throw my life away.

LADY RAN. What power directed thy unconscious
          tongue
To speak as thou hast done ? to name——

ANN.   I know not :
But since my words have made my mistress tremble,
I will speak so no more : but silent mix
My tears with hers.

LADY RAN.   No, thou shalt not be silent.
I'll trust thy faithful love, and thou shalt be
Henceforth th' instructed partner of my woes.
But what avails it ? Can thy feeble pity
Roll back the flood of never-ebbing time ?
Compel the earth and ocean to give up
Their dead alive ?

ANN.   What means my noble mistress ?

LADY RAN. Didst thou not ask what had my sor-
          rows been,
If I in early youth had lost a husband ?—
In the cold bosom of the earth is lodg'd,
Mangl'd with wounds, the husband of my youth ;
And in some cavern of the ocean lies
My child and his. ———

ANN.   O ! Lady, most rever'd !
The tale wrapt up in your amazing words
Deign to unfold.

LADY RAN.   Alas ! an ancient feud,
Hereditary evil, was the source
Of my misfortunes. Ruling fate decreed,
That my brave brother should in battle save
The life of Douglas' son, our house's foe :
The youthful warriors vow'd eternal friendship.

To see the vaunted sister of his friend,
Impatient, Douglas to Balarmo came,
Under a borrow'd name.—My heart he gain'd;
Nor did I long refuse the hand he begg'd:
My brother's presence authoriz'd our marriage.
Three weeks, three little weeks with wings of down,
Had o'er us flown, when my lov'd lord was call'd
To fight his father's battles; and with him,
In spite of all my tears did Malcolm go.
Scarce were they gone, when my stern sire was told
That the false stranger was Lord Douglas' son.
Frantic with rage the Baron drew his sword
And question'd me. Alone, forsaken, faint,
Kneeling beneath his sword, falt'ring I took
An oath equivocal, that I ne'er would
Wed one of Douglas' name. Sincerity!
Thou first of virtues, let no mortal leave
Thy onward path, altho' the earth should gape,
And from the gulph of hell destruction cry,
To take dissimulation's winding way.

ANN. Alas! how few of woman's fearful kind
Durst own a truth so hardy!

LADY RAN. The first truth
Is easiest to avow. This moral learn,
This precious moral from my tragic tale.——
In a few days the dreadful tidings came,
That Douglas and my brother both were slain.
My lord! my life! my husband!—mighty God!
What had I done to merit such affliction?

ANN. My dearest Lady! Many a tale of tears
I've listen'd to; but never did I hear
A tale so sad as this.

LADY RAN. In the first days
Of my distracting grief, I found myself—
As women wish to be who love their lords.

But who durst tell my father? The good priest
Who join'd our hands, my brother's ancient tutor,
With his lov'd Malcolm, in the battle fell:
They two alone were privy to the marriage.
On silence and concealment I resolv'd,
Till time should make my father's fortune mine.
That very night on which my son was born,
My nurse, the only confident I had,
Set out with him to reach her sister's house:
But nurse, nor infant have I ever seen,
Or heard of, Anna, since that fatal hour.
' My murder'd child!—had thy fond mother fear'd
' The loss of thee, she had loud fame defy'd,
' Despis'd her father's rage, her father's grief,
' And wander'd with thee thro' the scorning world.'
 ANN. Not seen or heard of! then perhaps he lives.
 LADY RAN. No. It was dark December: wind and rain
Had beat all night. Across the Carron lay
The destin'd road; and in its swelling flood
My faithful servant perish'd with my child.
' O! hapless son of a most hapless sire!—
' But they are both at rest; and I alone
' Dwell in this world of woe, condemn'd to walk,
' Like a guilt-troubl'd ghost, my painful rounds:'
Nor has despiteful fate permitted me
The comfort of a solitary sorrow.
Tho' dead to love, I was compell'd to wed
Randolph, who snatch'd me from a villain's arms;
And Randolph now possesses the domains,
That by Sir Malcolm's death on me devolv'd;
Domains, that should to Douglas' son have giv'n
A baron's title, and a baron's power.
' Such were my soothing thoughts, while I bewail'd
' The slaughter'd father of a son unborn.
' And when that son came, like a ray from heav'n,

' Which shines and disappears ; alas ! my child !
' How long did thy fond mother grasp the hope
' Of having thee, she knew not how, restor'd.
' Year after year hath worn her hope away ;
' But left still undiminish'd her desire.

 ' ANN. The hand that spins th' uneven thread of life,
' May smooth the length that's yet to come of yours.

 ' LADY RAN. Not in this world : I have consider'd well
' Its various evils, and on whom they fall.
' Alas ! how oft does goodness wound itself,
' And sweet affection prove the spring of woe !'
O ! had I dy'd when my lov'd husband fell !
Had some good angel op'd to me the book
Of Providence, and let me read my life,
My heart had broke, when I beheld the sum
Of ills, which one by one I have endur'd.

 ANN. That God, whose ministers good angels are,
Hath shut the book, in mercy to mankind ;
But we must leave this theme ; Glenalvon comes :
I saw him bend on you his thoughtful eyes,
And hitherwards he slowly stalks his way.

 LADY RAN. I will avoid him. An ungracious person
Is doubly irksome in an hour like this.

 ANN. Why speaks my lady thus of Randolph's heir?

 LADY RAN. Because he's not the heir of Randolph's
  virtues.
Subtle and shrewd he offers to mankind
An artificial image of himself :
And he with ease can vary to the taste
Of different men, its features. ' Self-denied,
' And master of his appetites he seems :
' But his fierce nature, like a fox chain'd up,
' Watches to seize unseen the wish'd-for prey.
' Never were vice and virtue pois'd so ill,
' As in Glenalvon's unrelenting mind.

Yet he is brave and politic in in war,
And stands aloft in these unruly times.
Why I describe him thus I'll tell hereafter.
Stay, and detain him till I reach the castle.
[*Exit* Lady Randolph.

ANN. O happiness! where art thou to be found?
I see thou dwellest not with birth and beauty,
Tho' grac'd with grandeur and in wealth arrry'd:
Nor dost thou, it would seem with virtue dwell;
Else had this gentle lady miss'd thee not.

Enter GLENALVON.

GLEN. What dost thou muse on, meditating maid?
Like some entranc'd and visionary seer,
On earth thou stand'st, thy thoughts ascend to heaven.

ANN. Wou'd that I were, e'en as thou say'st, a seer,
To have my doubts by heavenly vision clear'd!

GLEN. What dost thou doubt of? what hast thou to do
With subjects intricate? Thy youth, thy beauty,
Cannot be question'd. think of these good gifts;
And then thy contemplations will be pleasing.

ANN. Let women view yon monument of woe,
Then boast of beauty: who so fair as she?
But I must follow: this revolving day
Awakes the memory of her ancient woes.
[*Exit* Anna.

GLENALVON *solus*.

So!—Lady Randolph shuns me; by and by
I'll woo her as the lion wooes his brides.
The deed's a-doing now, that makes me lord
Of these rich vallies, and a chief of power.
The season is most apt: my sounding steps
Will not be heard amidst the din of arms.
Randolph has liv'd too long: his better fate
Had the ascendant once, and kept me down:
When I had feiz'd the dame, by chance he came,

Rescu'd, and had the lady for his labour.
I 'scap'd unknown: a slender consolation!
Heav'n is my witness that I do not love
To sow in peril, and let others reap
The jocund harvest. Yet I am not safe:
By love or something like it, stung, inflam'd,
Madly I blabb'd my passion to his wife,
And she has threaten'd to acquaint him of it.
The way of woman's will I do not know:
But well I know the Baron's wrath is deadly.
I will not live in fear: the man I dread
Is as a Dane to me: ay, and the man
Who stands betwixt me and my chief desire.
No bar but he: She has no kinsman near;
No brother in his sister's quarrel bold;
And for the righteous cause, a stranger's cause,
I know no chief that will defy Glenalvon.

ACT II.

SCENE,---*A Court*, etc.

Enter Servants *and* Stranger *at one door, and* LADY RANDOLPH *and* ANNA *at another.*

LADY RANDOLPH.

WHAT means this clamour? Stranger, speak secure;
Hast thou been wrong'd? have these rude men presum'd
To vex the weary traveller on his way?

 1st SERV. By us no stranger ever suffer'd wrong:
This man with outcry wild has call'd us forth;
So sore afraid he cannot speak his fears.

Enter LORD RANDOLPH *and a* Young Man, *with their swords drawn and bloody.*

LADY RAN. Not vain the stranger's fears! how fares my Lord.

RAN. That it fares well, thanks to this gallant youth,
Whose valour sav'd me from a wretched death!
As down the winding dale I walk'd alone,
At the cross way four armed men attack'd me;
Rovers, I judge, from the licentious camp;
Who would have quickly laid Lord Randolph low,
Had not this brave and generous stranger come,
Like my good angel, in the hour of fate,
And, mocking danger, made my foes his own.
They turn'd upon him; but his active arm
Struck to the ground, from whence they rose no more,
The fiercest two: the others fled amain,
And left him master of the bloody field.
Speak, Lady Randolph; upon beauty's tongue
Dwell accents pleasing to the brave and bold:
Speak, noble dame, and thank him for thy lord.

LADY RAN. My Lord, I cannot speak what now I feel.
My heart o'erflows with gratitude to heaven,
And to this noble youth, who, all unknown
To you and yours, deliberated not,
Nor paus'd at peril; but, humanely brave,
Fought on your fide against such fearful odds.
Have you yet learn'd of him whom we should thank?
Whom call the saviour of Lord Randolph's life?

RAN. I ask'd that question, and he answer'd not:
But I must know, who my deliverer is. [*To the stranger.*

STR. A low-born man, of parentage obscure,
Who nought can boast but his desire to be
A soldier, and to gain a name in arms.

RAN. Whoe'er thou art, thy spirit is ennobled
By the great King of kings! thou art ordain'd

And stampt a hero, by the sovereign hand
Of nature !—Blush not, flower of modesty
As well as valour, to declare thy birth.

   STR. My name is Norval : on the Grampian hills
My father feeds his flocks ; a frugal swain,
Whose constant cares were to increase his store,
And keep his only son, myself, at home :
For I had heard of battles, and I long'd
To follow to the field some warlike lord :
And heaven soon granted what my sire deny'd.
This moon which rose last night, round as my shield,
Had not yet fill'd her horns, when, by her light,
A band of fierce barbarians from the hills,
Rush'd like a torrent down upon the vale,
Sweeping our flocks and herds. The shepherds fled
For safety and for succour. I alone,
With bended bow, and quiver full of arrows,
Hover'd about the enemy, and mark'd
The road they took ; then hasted to my friends,
Whom, with a troop of fifty chosen men,
I met advancing. The pursuit I led,
Till we o'ertook the spoil-encumber'd foe.
We fought and conquer'd : E'er a sword was drawn,
An arrow from my bow had pierc'd their chief,
Who wore that day the arms which now I wear.
Returning home in triumph, I disdain'd
The shepherd's slothful life ; and having heard
That our good king had summon'd his bold peers
To lead their warriors to the Carron side,
I left my father's house, and took with me
A chosen servant to conduct my steps :—
Yon trembling coward, who forsook his master.
Journeying with this intent, I pass'd these towers,
And, heaven-directed, came this day to do
The happy deed that gilds my humble name.

RAN. He is as wise as brave. Was ever tale
With such a gallant modesty rehears'd?—
My brave deliv'rer! thou shalt enter now
A nobler list; and in a monarch's sight
Contend with princes for the prize of fame.
I will present thee to our Scottish king,
Whose valiant spirit ever valour lov'd.
Ha! my Matilda! wherefore starts that tear?

LADY RAN. I cannot say: for various affections,
And strangely mingled, in my bosom swell;
Yet each of them may well command a tear.
I joy that thou art safe; and I admire
Him and his fortunes, who hath wrought thy safety;
Yea, as my mind predicts, with thine his own.
Obscure and friendless, he the army sought,
Bent upon peril, in the range of death
Resolv'd to hunt for fame, and with his sword
To gain distinction which his birth deny'd.
In this attempt unknown he might have perish'd,
And gain'd, with all his valour, but oblivion.
Now, grac'd by thee, his virtue serves no more
Beneath despair. The soldier now of hope,
He stands conspicuous: fame and great renown
Are brought within the compass of his sword.
On this my mind reflected, whilst you spoke,
And bless'd the wonder-working Lord of heaven.

RAN. Pious and grateful ever are thy thoughts!
My deeds shall follow where thou point'st the way.
Next to myself, and equal to Glenalvon,
In honour and command shall Norval be.

NORV. I know not how to thank you. Rude I am
In speech and manners: Never till this hour
Stood I in such a presence; yet, my Lord,
There's something in my breast, which makes me bold
To say, that Norval ne'er will shame thy favour.

LADY RAN. I will be sworn thou wilt not. Thou shalt be
My knight ; and ever, as thou didst to-day,
With happy valour guard the life of Randolph.
 RAN. Well hast thou spoke. Let me forbid reply :
          [*To* Norval.
We are thy debtors still ; thy high desert
Oe'rtops our gratitude. I must proceed,
As was at first intended, to the camp.
Some of my train, I see, are speeding hither,
Impatient, doubtless, of their lord's delay.
Go with me, Norval, and thine eyes shall see
The chosen warriors of thy native land,
Who languish for the fight, and beat the air
With brandish'd swords.
 NORV.   Let us begone, my Lord.
 RAN. [*To Lady* Randolph.] About the time that
  the declining sun
Shall his broad orbit o'er yon hill suspend,
Expect us to return. This night once more
Within these walls I rest ; my tent I pitch
To-morrow in the field. Prepare the feast.
Free is his heart who for his country fights :
He in the eve of battle may resign
Himself to social pleasure : sweetest then,
When danger to a soldier's soul endears
The human joy that never may return.
      [*Exeunt* Randolph *and* Norval.
 LADY RAN. His parting words have struck a fatal
  truth.
O, Douglas! Douglas! tender was the time
When we two parted, ne'er to meet again !
How many years of anguish and despair
Has heaven annex'd to these swift-passing hours
Of love and fondness! Then my bosom's flame,

'Oft, as blown back by the rude breath of fear
'Return'd, and with redoubled ardour blaz'd.'

ANN. May gracious heaven pour the sweet balm of
 peace
Into the wounds that fester in your breast!
For earthly consolation cannot cure them.

LADY RAN. One only cure can heaven itself bestow;—
A grave—that bed in which the weary rest.
Wretch that I am! Alas! why am I so?
At every happy parent I repine!—
How blest the mother of yon gallant Norval!
She for a living husband bore her pains,
And heard him bless her when a man was born:
She nurs'd her smiling infant on her breast,
Tended the child, and rear'd the pleasing boy:
She, with affection's triumph, saw the youth
In grace and comeliness surpass his peers:
Whilst I to a dead husband bore a son,
And to the roaring waters gave my child.

ANN. Alas! alas! why will you thus resume
Your grief afresh? I thought that gallant youth
Would for a while have won you from your woe.
On him intent you gazed, with a look
Much more delighted than your pensive eye
Has deign'd on other objects to bestow.

LADY RAN. Delighted, say'st thou? Oh! even there
 mine eye
Found fuel for my life-consuming sorrow.
I thought, that had the son of Douglas liv'd,
He might have been like this young gallant stranger,
And pair'd with him in features and in shape.
In all endowments, as in years, I deem,
My boy with blooming Norval might have number'd.
Whilst thus I mus'd, a spark from fancy fell
On my sad heart, and kindled up a fondness

For this young stranger wand'ring from his home,
And like an orphan cast upon my care.
I will protect thee, (said I to myself,)
With all my power, and grace with all my favour.

ANN. Sure heaven will bless so gen'rous a resolve.
You must, my noble dame, exert your power;
You must awake: devices will be fram'd,
And arrows pointed at the breast of Norval.

LADY RAN. Glenalvon's false and crafty head will work
Against a rival in his kinsman's love,
If I deter him not: I only can.
Bold as he is, Glenalvon will beware
How he pulls down the fabric that I raise.
I'll be the artist of young Norval's fortune.
' 'Tis pleasing to admire! most apt was I
' To this affection in my better days;
' Though now I seem to you shrunk up, retir'd
' Within the narrow compass of my woe.
' Have you not sometimes seen an early flower
' Open its bud, and spread its silken leaves,
' To catch sweet airs, and odours to bestow;
' Then, by the keen blast nipt, pull in its leaves,
' And, though still living, die to scent and beauty?
' Emblem of me: affliction, like a storm,
' Hath kill'd the forward blossom of my heart.'

Enter GLENALVON.

GLEN. Where is my dearest kinsman, noble Randolph?
LADY RAN. Have you not heard, Glenalvon, of the
base—
GLEN. I have; and that the villains may not 'scape,
With a strong band I have begirt the wood;
If they lurk there, alive they shall be taken,
And torture force from them th' important secret,
Whether some foe of Randolph hir'd their swords,
Or if—

C

LADY RAN. That care becomes a kinsman's love.
I have a counsel for Glenalvon's ear. [*Exit* Anna.
GLEN. To him your counsels always are commands.
LADY RAN. I have not found so: thou art known to me.
GLEN. Known!
LADY RAN. And most certain is my cause of knowledge.
GLEN. What do you know? By the most blessed cross,
You much amaze me. No created being,
Yourself except, durst thus accost Glenalvon.
  LADY RAN. Is guilt so bold? and dost thou make a merit
Of thy pretended meekness? This to me,
Who, with a gentleness which duty blames,
Have hitherto conceal'd, what, if divulg'd,
Would make thee nothing; or, what's worse than that,
An outcast beggar, and unpity'd too:
For mortals shudder at a crime like thine.
  GLEN. Thy virtue awes me. First of womankind!
Permit me yet to say, that the fond man
Whom love transports beyond strict virtue's bounds,
If he is brought by love to misery,
In fortune ruin'd, as in mind forlorn,
Unpity'd cannot be. Pity's the alms
Which on such beggars freely is bestow'd;
For mortals know that love is still their lord,
And o'er their vain resolves advances still:
As fire, when kindl'd by our shepherds, moves
Through the dry heath before the fanning wind.
  LADY RAN. Reserve these accents for some other ear.
To love's apology I listen not.
Mark thou my words; for it is meet thou should'st.
His brave deliv'rer Randolph here retains.
Perhaps his presence may not please thee well;
But, at thy peril, practise ought against him.
Let not thy jealousy attempt to shake
And loosen the good root he has in Randolph;

Whose favourites I know thou hast supplanted.
Thou look'st at me, as if thou fain would'st pry
Into my heart. 'Tis open as my speech.
I give this early caution, and put on
The curb, before thy temper breaks away.
The friendless stranger my protection claims:
His friend I am, and be not thou his foe. [*Exit.*

GLEN. Child that I was, to start at my own sha-
    dow,
And be the shallow fool of coward conscience!
I am not what I have been : what I should be.
The darts of destiny have almost pierc'd
My marble heart. Had I one grain of faith
In holy legends and religious tales,
I should conclude there was an arm above
That fought against me, and malignant turn'd,
To catch myself, the subtle snare I set.
Why, rape and murder are not simple means!
Th' imperfect rape to Randolph gave a spouse;
And the intended murder introduc'd
A favourite to hide the sun from me;
And, worst of all, a rival. Burning hell!
This were thy centre, if I thought she lov'd him!
'Tis certain she contemns me ; nay commands me,
And waves the flag of her displeasure o'er me,
In his behalf. And shall I thus be brav'd?
Curb'd, as she calls it, by dame chastity?
Infernal fiends, if any fiends there are
More fierce than hate, ambition, and revenge,
Rise up, and fill my bosom with your fires
And policy remorseless! ' Chance may spoil
' A single aim ; but perseverance must
' Prosper at last. For chance and fate are words:
' Persistive wisdom is the fate of man.'
Darkly a project peers upon my mind,

Like the red moon when rising in the east,
Cross'd and divided by strange-colour'd clouds.
I'll seek the slave who came with Norval hither,
And for his cowardice was spurned from him.
I've known a follower's rankled bosom breed
Venom most fatal to his heedless lord.

ACT III.

SCENE,---*A Court*, etc. *as before.*

Enter ANNA.

Thy vassals, grief! great nature's order break,
And change the noon-tide to the midnight hour.
Whilst Lady Randolph sleeps, I will walk forth,
And taste the air that breathes on yonder bank.
Sweet may her slumbers be! Ye ministers
Of gracious heaven who love the human race,
Angels and seraphs who delight in goodness,
Forsake your skies, and to her couch descend!
There from her fancy chace those dismal forms
That haunt her waking; her sad spirit charm
With images celestial, such as please
The blest above upon their golden beds.

Enter Servant.

SERV. One of the vile assassins is secur'd.
We found the villain lurking in the wood:
With dreadful imprecations he denies
All knowledge of the crime. But this is not
His first essay: these jewels were conceal'd
In the most secret places of his garment;
Belike the spoils of some that he has murder'd.

ANN. Let me look on them. Ha! here is a heart,

The chosen crest of Douglas' valiant name!
These are no vulgar jewels. Guard the wretch.
[*Exit* Anna.

Enter Servants *with a* Prisoner.

PRIS. I know no more than does the child unborn
Of what you charge me with.
    1st SERV.   You say so, Sir!
But torture soon shall make you speak the truth.
Behold, the lady of Lord Randolph comes:
Prepare yourself to meet her just revenge.

Enter LADY RANDOLPH *and* ANNA.

ANN. Summon your utmost fortitude, before
You speak with him. Your dignity, your fame,
Are now at stake. Think of the fatal secret,
Which in a moment from your lips may fly.
    LADY RAN. Thou shalt behold me, with a desperate heart,
Hear how the infant perish'd. See, he kneels.
            [*The Prisoner kneels*.
    PRIS. Heaven bless that countenance so sweet and mild!
A judge like thee makes innocence more bold:
O save me, lady! from these cruel men,
Who have attack'd and seiz'd me; who accuse
Me of intended murder. As I hope
For mercy at the judgment seat of Heaven,
The tender lamb, that never nipt the grass,
Is not more innocent than I of murder.
    LADY RAN. Of this man's guilt what proof can ye produce?
    1st SERV. We found him lurking in the hollow glen.
When view'd and call'd upon, amaz'd he fled:
We overtook him, and enquir'd from whence
And what he was: He said he came from far,
And was upon his journey to the camp.

Not satisfied with this, we search'd his clothes,
And found these jewels, whose rich value plead
Most powerfully against him. Hard he seems,
And old in villainy. Permit us try
His stubborness against the torture's force.
   PRIS. O, gentle lady! by your lord's dear life,
Which these weak hands, I swear, did ne'er assail;
And by your children's welfare, spare my age!
Let not the iron tear my ancient joints,
And my grey hairs bring to the grave with pain.
   LADY RAN. Account for these; thine own they cannot be:
For these, I say: be stedfast to the truth;
Detected falsehood is most certain death.
        [Anna *removes the servants, and returns.*
   PRIS. Alas! I'm sore beset! Let never man,
For sake of lucre, sin against his soul!
Eternal justice is in this most just!
I, guiltless now, must former guilt reveal.
   LADY RAN. O! Anna, hear!—Once more I charge thee speak
The truth direct; for these to me foretel,
And certify a part of thy narration;
With which, if the remainder tallies not,
An instant and a dreadful death abides thee.
   PRIS. Then, thus adjur'd, I'll speak to you as just
As if you were the minister of heaven,
Sent down to search the secret sins of men.—
Some eighteen years ago I rented land
Of brave Sir Malcolm, then Balarmo's lord;
But falling to decay, his servants seiz'd
All that I had, and then turn'd me and mine,
(Four helpless infants and their weeping mother)
Out to the mercy of the winter winds.
A little hovel by the river's side

Receiv'd us: there hard labour, and the skill
In fishing, which was formerly my sport,
Supported life. Whilst thus we poorly liv'd,
One stormy night, as I remember well,
The wind and rain beat hard upon our roof:
Red came the river down, and loud and oft
The angry spirit of the water shriek'd.
At the dead hour of night was heard the cry
Of one in jeopardy. I rose, and ran
To where the circling eddy of a pool,
Beneath the ford, us'd oft to bring within
My reach, whatever floating thing the stream
Had caught. The voice was ceas'd; the person lost:
But, looking sad and earnest on the waters,
By the moon's light I saw, whirl'd round and round,
A basket: soon I drew it to the bank,
And, nestled curious, there an infant lay.
 LADY RAN. Was he alive?
 PRIS.   He was.
 LADY RAN.   Inhuman that thou art!
How could'st thou kill what waves and tempests spar'd.?
 PRIS. I was not so inhuman.
 LADY RAN.   Didst thou not?
 ANN. My noble mistress, you are mov'd too much.
This man has not the aspect of stern murder:
Let him go on; and you, I hope, will hear
Good tidings of your kinsman's long lost child.
 PRIS. The needy man who has known better days,
One whom distress has spited at the world,
Is he whom tempting fiends would pitch upon
To do such deeds as make the prosperous men
Lift up their hands and wonder who could do them.
And such a man was I: a man declin'd,
Who saw no end of black adversity:

Yet, for the wealth of kingdoms, I would not
Have touch'd that infant with a hand of harm.
  LADY RAN. Ha! dost thou say so? Then perhaps he
    lives!
  PRIS. Not many days ago he was alive.
  LADY RAN. O God of heaven! Did he then die so
    lately?.
  PRIS. I did not say he died; I hope he lives.
Not many days ago these eyes beheld
Him, flourishing in youth, and health, and beauty.
  LADY RAN. Where is he now?
  PRIS.   Alas! I know not where.
  LADY RAN. Oh, fate! I fear thee still. Thou riddler,
    speak
Direct and clear, else I will search thy soul.
  ' ANN. Permit me, ever honour'd! Keen impatience,
' Though hard to be restrain'd, defeats itself.—'
Pursue thy story with a faithful tongue
To the last hour that thou didst keep the child.
  PRIS. Fear not my faith, though I must speak my
    shame.
Within the cradle where the infant lay
Was stow'd a mighty store of gold and jewels;
Tempted by which, we did resolve to hide,
From all the world this wonderful event,
And like a peasant breed the noble child.
That none might mark the change of our estate,
We left the country, travell'd to the north,
Bought flocks and herds, and gradually brought forth
Our secret wealth. But God's all-seeing eye
Beheld our avarice, and smote us sore.
For, one by one, all our own children died;
And he, the stranger, sole remain'd the heir
Of what indeed was his. Fain then would I,
Who with a father's fondness lov'd the boy,

Have trusted him, now in the dawn of youth,
With his own secret: but my anxious wife,
Foreboding evil, never would consent.
Meanwhile the stripling grew in years and beauty;
And, as we oft observ'd, he bore himself,
Not as the offspring of our cottage blood;
For nature will break out: mild with the mild,
But with the forward he was fierce as fire,
And night and day he talk'd of war and arms.
I set myself against his warlike bent;
But all in vain; for when a desperate band
Of robbers from the savage mountains came—

LADY RAN. Eternal Providence! What is thy name?

PRIS. My name is NORVAL; and my name he bears.

LADY RAN. 'Tis he; 'tis he himself! it is my son!
O, sovereign mercy! 'twas my child I saw!—
No wonder, Anna, that my bosom burn'd.

ANN. Just are your transports: 'ne'er was woman's heart
' Prov'd with such fierce extremes. High-fated dame!'
But yet remember that you are beheld
By servile eyes: your gestures may be seen
Impassion'd strange; perhaps your words o'erheard.

LADY RAN. Well dost thou counsel, Anna, Heaven bestow
On me that wisdom which my state requires!

' ANN. The moments of deliberation pass,
' And soon you must resolve. This useful man
' Must be dismiss'd in safety, e'er my lord
' Shall with his brave deliverer return.'

PRIS. If I, amidst astonishment and fear,
Have of your words and gestures rightly judg'd,
Thou art the daughter of my ancient master;
The child I rescu'd from the flood is thine.

LADY RAN. With thee dissimulation now were vain.

I am indeed the daughter of Sir Malcolm;
The child thou rescu'dst from the flood is mine.

PRIS. Blest be the hour that made me a poor man!
My poverty has sav'd my master's house!

LADY RAN. Thy words surprise me: sure thou dost
not feign!
The tear stands in thine eye: such love from thee
Sir Malcolm's house deserv'd not, if aright
Thou told'st the story of thy own distress.

PRIS. Sir Malcolm of our barons was the flower;
The fastest friend, the best, the kindest master.
But ah! he knew not of my sad estate.
After that battle, where his gallant son,
Your own brave brother, fell, the good old lord
Grew desperate and reckless of the world:
And never, as he erst was wont, went forth
To overlook the conduct of his servants.
By them I was thrust out, and them I blame.
May heaven so judge me as I judg'd my master!
And God so love me as I love his race!

LADY RAN. His race shall yet reward thee. On thy
faith
Depends the fate of thy lov'd master's house.
Rememb'rest thou a little lonely hut,
That like a holy hermitage appears
Among the clefts of Carron?

PRIS. I remember
The cottage of the clefts.

LADY RAN. 'Tis that I mean.
There dwells a man of venerable age,
Who in my father's service spent his youth:
Tell him I sent thee, and with him remain,
'Till I shall call upon thee to declare,
Before the king and nobles what thou now
To me hast told. No more but this, and thou

Shalt live in honour all thy future days;
Thy son so long shall call thee father still,
And all the land shall bless the man who sav'd
The son of Douglas, and Sir Malcolm's heir.
Remember well my words; if thou shouldst meet
Him whom thou call'st thy son, still call him so;
And mention nothing of his nobler father.

PRIS. Fear not that I shall mar so fair an harvest,
By putting in my sickle ere 'tis ripe.
Why did I leave my home and ancient dame?
To find the youth, to tell him all I knew,
And make him wear these jewels in his arms,
Which might, I thought, be challeng'd, and so bring
To light the secret of his noble birth.

[*Lady* Randolph *goes towards the servants.*

LADY RAN. This man is not the assassin you suspected,
Tho' chance combin'd some likelihoods against him.
He is the faithful bearer of the jewels
To their right owner, whom in haste he seeks.
'Tis meet that you should put him on his way,
Since your mistaken zeal hath dragg'd him hither.

[*Exeunt Stranger and Servants.*

My faithful Anna! dost thou share my joy?
I know thou dost.—Unparallel'd event!
Reaching from heaven to earth, Jehovah's arm
Snatch'd from the waves, and brings to me my son!
Judge of the widow, and the orphan's father,
Accept a widow's and a mother's thanks
For such a gift!—What does my Anna think
Of the young eaglet of a valiant nest?
How soon he gaz'd on bright and burning arms,
Spurn'd the low dunghill where his fate had thrown
    him,
And tower'd up to the region of his sire.

ANN. How fondly did your eyes devour the boy!

Mysterious nature, with the unseen cord
Of powerful instinct, drew you to your own.

LADY RAN. The ready story of his birth believ'd
Suppress'd my fancy quite ; nor did he owe
To any likeness my so sudden favour :
But now I long to see his face again,
Examine every feature, and find out
The lineaments of Douglas, or my own.
But most of all I long to let him know
Who his true parents are, to clasp his neck,
And tell him all the story of his father.

ANN. With wary caution you must bear yourself
In public, lest your tenderness break forth,
And in observers stir conjectures strange.
' For if a cherub in the shape of woman
' Should walk this world, yet defamation would,
' Like a vile cur, bark at the angel's train.—'
To-day the baron started at your tears.

LADY RAN. He did so, Anna ! Well thy mistress knows
If the least circumstance, mote of offence,
Should touch the baron's eye, his sight would be
With jealousy disorder'd.   But the more
It does behove me instant to declare
The birth of Douglas, and assert his rights.
This night I purpose with my son to meet,
Reveal the secret, and consult with him :
For wise he is, or my fond judgment errs.
As he does now, so look'd his noble father,
Array'd in nature's ease : his mien, his speech,
Were sweetly simple, and full oft deceiv'd
Those trivial mortals who seem always wise.
But, when the matter match'd his mighty mind,
Up rose the hero ; on his piercing eye
Sat observation ; on each glance of thought
Decision follow'd, as the thunderbolt

Pursues the flash.

ANN. That demon haunts you still:
Behold Glenalvon.

LADY RAN. Now I shun him not.
This day I brav'd him in behalf of Norval;
Perhaps too far; at least my nicer fears
For Douglas thus interpret.

Enter GLENALVON.

GLEN. Noble dame!
The hov'ring Dane at last his men hath landed:
No band of pirates; but a mighty host,
That come to settle where their valour conquers;
To win a country, or to lose themselves.

LADY RAN. But whence comes this intelligence, Glenalvon?

GLEN. A nimble courier sent from yonder camp,
To hasten up the chieftains of the north,
Inform'd me, as he past, that the fierce Dane
Had on the eastern coast of Lothian landed,
' Near to that place where the sea-rock immense,
' Amazing Bass! looks o'er a fertile land.

' LADY RAN. Then must this western army march to join
'The warlike troops that guard Edina's tow'rs.

' GLEN. Beyond all question. If impairing time
' Has not effac'd the image of a place,
' Once perfect in my breast, there is a wild
' Which lies to westward of that mighty rock,
' And seems by nature formed for the camp
' Of water-wafted armies, whose chief strength
' Lies in firm foot, unflank'd with warlike horse:
' If martial skill directs the Danish lords,
' There inaccessible their army lies
' To our swift-scow'ring horse; the bloody field
' Must man to man, and foot to foot be fought.'

D

LADY RAN. How many mothers shall bewail their sons!
How many widows weep their husbands slain!
Ye dames of Denmark! even for you I feel,
Who, sadly sitting on the sea-beat shore,
Long look for lords that never shall return.

GLEN. Oft has th' unconquer'd Caledonian sword
Widow'd the north. The children of the slain
Come, as I hope, to meet their father's fate.
The monster War, with her infernal brood,
Loud-yelling fury, and life-ending pain,
Are objects suited to Glenalvon's soul.
Scorn is more grievous than the pains of death;
Reproach more piercing than the pointed sword.

LADY RAN. I scorn thee not, but when I ought to scorn;
Nor e'er reproach, but when insulted virtue
Against audacious vice asserts herself.
I own thy worth, Glenalvon; none more apt
Than I to praise thine eminence in arms,
And be the echo of thy martial fame.
No longer vainly feed a guilty passion:
Go and pursue a lawful mistress, Glory!
Upon the Danish crests redeem thy fault,
And let thy valour be the shield of Randolph.

GLEN. One instant stay, and hear an alter'd man.
When beauty pleads for virtue, vice abash'd
Flies its own colours, and goes o'er to virtue.
I am your convert; time will shew how truly:
Yet one immediate proof I mean to give—
That youth, for whom your ardent zeal to-day
Somewhat too haughtily defy'd your slave,
Amidst the shock of armies I'll defend,
And turn death from him with a guardian arm.
' Sedate by use, my bosom maddens not

'At the tumultuous uproar of the field.'

LADY RAN. Act thus, Glenalvon, and I am thy friend:
But that's thy least reward. Believe me, Sir,
The truly generous is the truly wise;
And he who loves not others, lives unblest.
[*Exit* Lady Randolph.

GLEN. Amen! and virtue is its own reward!—
I think that I have hit the very tone
In which she loves to speak. Honey'd assent,
How pleasant art thou to the taste of man,
And woman also! Flattery direct
Rarely disgusts. They little know mankind
Who doubt its operations. 'Tis my key,
And opes the wicket of the human heart.
How far I have succeeded now, I know not:
Yet I incline to think her stormy virtue
Is lull'd a while. 'Tis her alone I fear.
Whilst she and Randolph live, and live in faith
And amity, uncertain is my tenure.
' Fate o'er my head suspends disgrace and death,
' By that weak hair, a peevish female's will.
' I am not idle; but the ebbs and flows
' Of fortune's tide cannot be calculated.'
That slave of Norval's I have found most apt!
I shew'd him gold, and he has pawn'd his soul
To say and swear whatever I suggest.
Norval, I'm told, has that alluring look,
'Twixt man and woman, which I have observ'd
To charm the nicer and fantastic dames,
Who are, like Lady Randolph, full of virtue.
In raising Randolph's jealousy, I may
But point him to the truth. He seldom errs,
Who thinks the worst he can of womankind. [*Exit.*

ACT IV.

SCENE,---*A Court*, etc. *as before.* *Flourish of Trumpets.*

Enter RANDOLPH *attended.*

RAN. SUMMON an hundred horse by break of day,
To wait our pleasure at the castle gate.

Enter LADY RANDOLPH.

LADY RAN. Alas! my Lord! I've heard unwelcome
news;
The Danes are landed.

RAN. Ay; no inroad this
Of the Northumbrian bent to take a spoil:
No sportive war; no tournament essay
Of some young knight resolv'd to break a spear,
And stain with hostile blood his maiden arms.
The Danes are landed: We must beat them back,
Or live the slaves of Denmark.

LADY RAN. Dreadful times!

RAN. The fenceless villages are all forsaken:
The trembling mothers, and their children lodg'd,
In wall-girt towers and castles; whilst the men
Retire indignant. Yet, like broken waves,
They but retire more awful to return.

LADY RAN. Immense, as fame reports, the Danish host!

RAN. Were it as numerous as loud fame reports,
An army knit like ours would pierce it through:
Brothers, that shrink not from each other's side,
And fond companions, fill our warlike files:
For his dear offspring, and the wife he loves,
The husband and the fearless father arm.
In vulgar breasts heroic ardour burns,
And the poor peasant mates his daring lord.

LADY RAN. Men's minds are temper'd, like their
    swords, for war :
Lovers of danger, on destruction's brink
They joy to rear erect their daring forms.
Hence early graves ; hence, the lone widow's life ;
And the sad mother's grief-embitter'd age.——
Where is our gallant guest ?
    RAN.   Down in the vale
I left him, managing a fiery steed,
Whose stubborness had foil'd the strength and skill
Of every rider. But behold he comes
In earnest conversation with Glenalvon.

        Enter NORVAL *and* GLENALVON.

Glenalvon ! with the lark arise ; go forth,
And lead my troops that lie in yonder vale :
Private I travel to the royal camp.
Norval, thou goest with me. But say, young man!
Where didst thou learn so to discourse of war,
And in such terms, as I o'erheard to-day ?
War is no village science, nor its phrase
A language taught among the shepherd swains.
    NORV. Small is the skill my Lord delights to praise
In him he favours.—Hear from whence it came.
Beneath a mountain's brow, the most remote
And inaccessible by shepherds trod,
In a deep cave, dug by no mortal hand,
A hermit liv'd ; a melancholy man,
Who was the wonder of our wand'ring swains.
Austere and lonely, cruel to himself,
Did they report him : The cold earth his bed,
Water his drink, his food the shepherd's alms.
I went to see him, and my heart was touch'd
With reverence and with pity. Mild he spake,
And, entering on discoure, such stories told
As made me oft revisit his sad cell ;

For he had been a soldier in his youth,
And fought in famous battles, when the peers
Of Europe, by the bold Godfredo led,
Against th' usurping infidel display'd
The blessed cross, and won the Holy Land.
Pleas'd with my admiration, and the fire
His speech struck from me, the old man would shake
His years away, and act his young encounters:
Then, having shew'd his wounds, he'd sit him down,
And all the live-long day discourse of war,
To help my fancy, in the smooth green turf
He cut the figures of the marshall'd hosts;
Describ'd the motions, and explain'd the use
Of the deep column, and the lengthen'd line,
The square, the crescent, and the phalanx firm:
For all that Saracen or Christian knew
Of war's vast art, was to this hermit known.

RAN. Why did this soldier in a desert hide
Those qualities that should have grac'd a camp?

NORV. That too at last I learned. Unhappy man!
Returning homewards by Messina's port,
Loaded with wealth and honours bravely won,
A rude and boist'rous captain of the sea
Fasten'd a quarrel on him. Fierce they fought:
The stranger fell, and with his dying breath
Declar'd his name and lineage—Mighty Power!
The soldier cried, my brother! O, my brother!

LADY RAN. His brother!

NORV.   Yes; of the same parents born:
His only brother. They exchang'd forgiveness;
And happy, in my mind, was he that dy'd;
For many deaths has the survivor suffer'd.
In the wild desert on a rock he sits,
Or on some nameless stream's untrodden banks,
And ruminates all day his dreadful fate.

At times, alas! not in his perfect mind,
Holds dialogues with his lov'd brother's ghost;
And oft each night forsakes his sullen couch,
To make sad orisons for him he slew.

    LADY RAN. To what mysterious woes are mortals
        born!—
In this dire tragedy, were there no more
Unhappy persons? Did the parents live?

    NORV. No; they were dead: kind heav'n had clos'd
        their eyes
Before their son had shed his brother's blood.

    LADY RAN. Hard is his fate! for he was not to blame.
There is a destiny in this strange world,
Which oft decrees an undeserved doom:
Let schoolmen tell us why.—From whence these
        sounds?   [*Trumpets at a distance*
        Enter an Officer.

    OFF. My lord, the trumpets of the troops of Lorn:
The valiant leader hails the noble Randolph.

    RAN. Mine ancient guest! does he the warriors lead?
Has Denmark rous'd the brave old knight to arms?

    OFF. No: worn with warfare, he resigns the sword.
His eldest hope, the valiant John of Lorn,
Now leads his kindred bands.

    RAN.   Glenalvon, go:
With hospitality's most strong request
Entreat the chief.   [*Exit* Glenalvon.

    OFF.   My lord! requests are vain.
He urges on, impatient of delay,
Stung with the tidings of the foe's approach.

    RAN. May victory sit on the warrior's plume!
Bravest of men! his flocks and herds are safe;
Remote from war's alarms his pastures lie,
By mountains inaccessible secur'd;
Yet foremost he into the plain descends,

Eager to bleed in battles not his own.
Such were the heroes of the ancient world;
Contemners they of indolence and gain;
But still, for love of glory and of arms,
Prone to encounter peril, and to lift
Against each strong antagonist the spear—
I'll go and press the hero to my breast.
[*Exit* Randolph.

LADY RAN. The soldier's loftiness, the pride and pomp
Investing awful war, Norval! I see,
Transport thy youthful mind.

NORV. Ah! should they not?
Blest be the hour I left my father's house!
I might have been a shepherd all my days,
And stole obscurely to a peasant's grave.
Now, if I live, with mighty chiefs I stand;
And, if I fall, with noble dust I lie.

LADY RAN. There is a gen'rous spirit in thy breast,
That could have well sustain'd a prouder fortune.
This way with me: under yon spreading beech,
Unseen, unheard, by human eye or ear,
I will amaze thee with a wond'rous tale.

NORV. Let there be danger, lady, with the secret,
That I may hug it to my grateful heart,
And prove my faith. Command my sword, my life;
These are the sole possessions of poor Norval.

LADY RAN. Know'st thou these gems?

NORV. Durst I believe mine eyes,
I'd say I knew them, and they were my father's.

LADY RAN. Thy father's, say'st thou? Ah! they were thy father's!

NORV. I saw them once, and curiously enquir'd
Of both my parents, whence such splendor came?
But I was check'd, and more could never learn.

LADY RAN. Then learn of me, thou art not Norval's son.
NORV. Not Norval's son!
LADY RAN. Nor of a shepherd sprung.
NORV. Lady, who am I then?
LADY RAN. Noble thou art;
For noble was thy sire!
NORV. I will believe—
O, tell me farther! Say, who was my father?
LADY RAN. DOUGLAS!
NORV. Lord Douglas! whom to-day I saw?
LADY RAN. His younger brother.
NORV. And in yonder camp?
LADY RAN. Alas!
NORV. You make me tremble—Sighs and tears!—
Lives my brave father?
LADY RAN. Ah! too brave indeed:
He fell in battle e'er thyself was born.
NORV. Ah me, unhappy! e'er myself was born!—
But does my mother live? I may conclude
From my own fate, her portion has been sorrow.
LADY RAN. She lives; but wastes her life in constant
woe,
Weeping her husband slain, her infant lost.
NORV. You that are skill'd so well in the sad story
Of my unhappy parents, and with tears
Bewail their destiny, now have compassion
Upon the offspring of the friends you lov'd;
O! tell me who and where my mother is.
Oppress'd by a base world, perhaps she bends
Beneath the weight of other ills than grief;
And, desolate, implores of heaven the aid
Her son should give. It is, it must be so—
Your countenance confesses that she's wretched.
O! tell me her condition! Can the sword—
Who shall resist me in a parent's cause?

LADY RAN. Thy virtue ends her woes—My son!
my son!
I am thy mother, and the wife of Douglas!
[*Falls upon his neck.*

NORV. O heav'n and earth! how wondrous is my fate!
Art thou my mother? Ever let me kneel.

LADY RAN. Image of Douglas! fruit of fatal love!
All that I owe thy sire, I pay to thee.

NORV. Respect and admiration still possess me,
Checking the love and fondness of a son:
Yet I was filial to my humble parents.
But did my sire surpass the rest of men,
As thou excellest all of womankind?

LADY RAN. Arise, my son! In me thou dost behold
The poor remains of beauty once admir'd!
The autumn of my days is come already;
For sorrow made my summer haste away.
Yet in my prime I equall'd not thy father:
His eyes were like the eagle's, yet sometimes
Liker the dove's; and, as he pleas'd, he won
All hearts with softness, or with spirit aw'd.

NORV. How did he fall? Sure 'twas a bloody field
When Douglas died. O! I have much to ask.

LADY RAN. Hereafter thou shalt hear the lengthen'd
tale
Of all thy father's and thy mother's woes.
At present this: Thou art the rightful heir
Of yonder castle, and the wide domains
Which now Lord Randolph, as my husband, holds.
But thou shalt not be wrong'd; I have the power
To right thee still. Before the king I'll kneel;
And call Lord Douglas to protect his blood.

NORV. The blood of Douglas will protect itself.

LADY RAN. But we shall need both friends and favour,
boy,

To wrest thy lands and lordship from the gripe
Of Randolph and his kinsman. Yet I think
My tale will move each gentle heart to pity;
My life incline the virtuous to believe.

NORV. To be the son of Douglas, is to me
Inheritance enough. Declare my birth,
And in the field I'll seek for fame and fortune.

LADY RAN. Thou dost not know what perils and injustice
Await the poor man's valour. O, my son!
The noblest blood of all the land's abash'd,
Having no lacquey but pale poverty.
Too long hast thou been thus attended, Douglas!
Too long hast thou been deem'd a peasant's child.
The wanton heir of some inglorious chief
Perhaps has scorn'd thee in the youthful sports;
Whilst thy indignant spirit swell'd in vain!
Such contumely thou no more shalt bear;
But how I purpose to redress thy wrongs
Must be hereafter told. Prudence directs
That we should part before yon chiefs return.
Retire; and from thy rustic follower's hand
Receive a billet, which thy mother's care,
Anxious to see thee, dictated before
This casual opportunity arose
Of private conference. Its purport mark;
For as I there appoint, we meet again.
Leave me, my son! and frame thy manners still
To Norval's, not to noble Douglas' state.

NORV. I will remember. Where is Norval now?
That good old man.

LADY RAN. At hand, conceal'd he lies,
An useful witness. But beware, my son,
Of yon Glenalvon; In his guilty breast

Resides a villain's shrewdness, ever prone
To false conjecture. He hath griev'd my heart.

NORV. Has he, indeed? Then let yon false Glenalvon
Beware of me.   [*Exit* Douglas.

LADY RAN. There burst the smother'd flame.
O! thou all righteous and eternal King!
Who Father of the fatherless art call'd,
Protect my son! Thy inspiration, Lord!
Hath fill'd his bosom with that sacred fire
Which in the breast of his forefathers burn'd:
Set him on high, like them, that he may shine
The star and glory of his native land!
Then let the minister of death descend,
And bear my willing spirit to its place.—
Yonder they come. How do bad women find
Unchanging aspects to conceal their guilt,
When I, by reason and by justice urg'd,
Full hardly can dissemble with these men
In nature's pious cause?

Enter RANDOLPH *and* GLENALVON.

RAN. Yon gallant chief,
Of arms enamour'd, all repose disclaims.
LADY RAN. Be not, my Lord, by his example sway'd.
Arrange the business of to-morrow now;
And when you enter, speak of war no more.
                                    [*Exit* Lady Randolph.

RAN. 'Tis so, by Heav'n! her mien, her voice, her eye,
And her impatience to be gone, confirm it.
GLEN. He parted from her now: Behind the mount,
Amongst the trees, I saw him glide along.
RAN. For sad sequester'd virtue she's renown'd!
GLEN. Most true, my lord.
RAN.   Yet this distinguish'd dame
Invites a youth, th' acquaintance of a day,
Alone to meet her at the midnight hour.

This assignation (*shews a letter*) the assassin freed,
Her manifest affection for the youth,
Might breed suspicion in a husband's brain,
Whose gentle consort all for love had wedded :
Much more in mine. Matilda never lov'd me.
Let no man, after me, a woman wed,
Whose heart he knows he has not ; though she brings
A mine of gold, a kingdom for her dowry :
For, let her seem like the night's shadowy queen,
Cold and contemplative,—he cannot trust her :
She may, she will, bring shame and sorrow on him ;
The worst of sorrows, and the worst of shames !

   GLEN. Yield not, my lord, to such afflicting thoughts;
But let the spirit of an husband sleep,
Till your own senses make a sure conclusion.
This billet must to blooming Norval go.
At the next turn awaits my trusty spy :
I'll give it him refitted for his master.
In the close thicket take your secret stand :
The moon shines bright, and your own eyes may judge
Of their behaviour.

   RAN.   Thou dost counsel well.

   GLEN. Permit me now to make one slight essay.
Of all the trophies which vain mortals boast,
By wit, by valour, or by wisdom won,
The first and fairest, in a young man's eye,
Is woman's captive heart. Successful love
With glorious fumes intoxicates the mind !
And the proud conqueror in triumph moves,
Air-born, exalted above vulgar men.

   RAN. And what avails this maxim ?

   GLEN.   Much, my lord!
Withdraw a little : I'll accost young Norval,
And with ironical derisive counsel
Explore his spirit. If he is no more

Than humble Norval, by thy favour rais'd,
Brave as he is, he'll shrink astonish'd from me:
But if he be the favourite of the fair,
Lov'd by the first of Caledonia's dames,
He'll turn upon me, as the lion turns
Upon the hunter's spear.

RAN. 'Tis shrewdly thought.

GLEN. When we grow loud, draw near. But let my lord
His rising wrath restrain. [*Exit* Randolph.

GLEN. 'Tis strange, by heaven!
That she should run full tilt her fond career,
To one so little known. She too, that seem'd
Pure as the winter stream, when ice emboss'd
Whitens its course. Even I did think her chaste,
Whose charity exceeds not. Precious sex!
Whose deeds lascivious pass Glenalvon's thoughts!

Enter NORVAL.

His port I love; he's in a proper mood
To chide the thunder, if at him it roar'd.
Has Norval seen the troops?

NORV. The setting sun
With yellow radiance lighten'd all the vale;
And as the warriors mov'd, each polish'd helm,
Corslet, or spear, glanc'd back his gilded beams.
The hill they climb'd; and, halting at its top,
Of more than mortal size, tow'ring, they seem'd
An host angelic, clad in burning arms.

GLEN. Thou talk'st it well; no leader of our host
In sounds more lofty speaks of glorious war.

NORV. If I shall e'er acquire a leader's name,
My speech will be less ardent. Novelty
Now prompts my tongue, and youthful admiration
Vents itself freely; since no part is mine
Of praise pertaining to the great in arms.

GLEN. You wrong yourself, brave Sir; your martial
  deeds
Have rank'd thee with the great; but mark me Norval;
Lord Randolph's favour now exalts your youth
Above his veterans of famous service.
Let me, who know these soldiers, counsel you :
Give them all honour; seem not to command;
Else they will scarcely brook your late sprung power,
Which nor alliance props, nor birth adorns.
  NORV. Sir, I have been accustom'd all my days
To hear and speak the plain and simple truth :
And though I have been told that there are men
Who borrow friendship's tongue to speak their scorn,
Yet in such language I am little skill'd.
Therefore I thank Glenalvon for his counsel,
Although it sounded harshly. Why remind
Me of my birth obscure? Why slur my power
With such contemptuous terms?
  GLEN.   I did not mean
To gall your pride, which now I see is great.
  NORV. My pride!
  GLEN.   Suppress it as you wish to prosper.
Your pride's excessive. Yet, for Randolph's sake,
I will not leave you to its rash direction.
If thus you swell, and frown at high-born men,
Will high-born men endure a shepherd's scorn?
  NORV. A shepherd's scorn!
  GLEN.   Yes; if you presume
To bend on soldiers these disdainful eyes,
As if you took the measure of their minds,
And said in secret, you're no match for me;
What will become of you?
  NORV.   If this were told!— ·[*Aside*,
Hast thou no fears for thy presumptuous self?
  GLEN. Ha! dost thou threaten me?

NORV. Didst thou not hear?
GLEN. Unwillingly I did; a nobler foe
Had not been question'd thus. But such as thee—
NORV. Whom dost thou think me?
GLEN. Norval.
NORV. So I am—
And who is Norval in Glenalvon's eyes?
GLEN. A peasant's son, a wandering beggar-boy;
At best no more, even if he speaks the truth.
NORV. False as thou art, dost thou suspect my truth?
GLEN. Thy truth! thou'rt all a lie; and false as hell
Is the vain glorious tale thou toldst to Randolph.
NORV. If I were chain'd, unarm'd, and bedrid old,
Perhaps I should revile: but as I am,
I have no tongue to rail. The humble Norval
Is of a race who strive not but with deeds.
Did I not fear to freeze thy shallow valour,
And make thee sink too soon beneath my sword,
I'd tell thee—what thou art: I know thee well.
GLEN. Dost thou not know Glenalvon, born to command
Ten thousand slaves like thee?——
NORV. Villain, no more!
Draw and defend thy life. I did design
To have defy'd thee in another cause:
But heaven accelerates its vengeance on thee.
Now for my own and Lady Randolph's wrongs.

Enter RANDOLPH.

RAN. Hold, I command you both. The man that stirs
Makes me his foe.
NORV. Another voice than thine
That threat had vainly sounded, noble Randolph.
GLEN. Hear him, my Lord; he's wond'rous condescending!

Mark the humility of shepherd Norval!

NORV. Now you may scoff in safety. [*Sheaths his sword.*

RAN. Speak not thus,
Taunting each other; but unfold to me
The cause of quarrel; then I judge betwixt you.

NORV. Nay, my good lord, tho' I revere you much,
My cause I plead not, nor demand your judgment.
I blush to speak; I will not, cannot speak
Th' opprobrious words that I from him have borne.
To the liege lord of my dear native land
I owe a subject's homage: but ev'n him
And his high arbitration I'd reject.
Within my bosom reigns another lord;
Honour, sole judge and umpire of itself.
If my free speech offend you, noble Randolph,
Revoke your favours; and let Norval go
Hence as he came, alone, but not dishonour'd.

RAN. Thus far I'll mediate with impartial voice.
The ancient foe of Caledonia's land
Now waves his banners o'er her frighted fields.
Suspend your purpose, till your country's arms
Repel the bold invader: then decide
The private quarrel.

GLEN. I agree to this.

NORV. And I.

Enter Servant.

SERV. The banquet waits.

RAN. We come. [*Exit with servant.*

GLEN. Norval,
Let not our variance mar the social hour,
Nor wrong the hospitality of Randolph.
Nor frowning anger, nor yet wrinkl'd hate,
Shall stain my countenance. Smooth thou thy brow;
Nor let our strife disturb the gentle dame.

NOR. Think not so lightly, Sir, of my resentment:
When we contend again, our strife is mortal.

ACT V.

SCENE,---*The Wood.*

Enter DOUGLAS.

THIS is the place, the centre of the grove;
Here stands the oak, the monarch of the wood.
How sweet and solemn is this midnight scene!
The silver moon, unclouded, holds her way
Through skies where I could count each little star.
The fanning west wind scarcely stirs the leaves.
The river, rushing o'er its pebbled bed,
Imposes silence with a stilly sound.
In such a place as this, at such an hour,
If ancestry can be in ought believ'd,
Descending spirits have convers'd with man,
And told the secrets of the world unknown.

Enter OLD NORVAL.

OLD NORV. 'Tis he. But what if he should chide me hence?
His just reproach I fear. [Douglas *turns and sees him*]
Forgive, forgive.
Can'st thou forgive the man, the selfish man,
Who bred Sir Malcolm's heir a shepherd's son?

DOUG. Kneel not to me: thou art my father still;
Thy wish'd-for presence now completes my joy.
Welcome to me; my fortunes thou shalt share,
And ever-honour'd with thy Douglas live.

O. NORV. And dost thou call me father? O my son!
I think that I could die to make amends

For the great wrong I did thee. 'Twas my crime
Which in the wilderness so long conceal'd
The blossom of thy youth.

DOUG.   Not worse the fruit,
That in the wilderness the blossom blow'd.
Amongst the shepherds, in the humble cot,
I learn'd some lessons, which I'll not forget
When I inhabit yonder lofty towers.
I, who was once a swain, will ever prove
The poor man's friend; and when my vassals bow,
Norval shall smooth the crested pride of Douglas.

O. NORV. Let me but live to see thine exaltation!—
Yet grievous are my fears. O leave this place,
And those unfriendly towers.

DOUG.   Why should I leave them?

O. NORV. Lord Randolph and his kinsman seek your life.

DOUG. How know'st thou that?

O. NORV.   I will inform you how.
When evening came, I left the sacred place
Appointed for me by your mother's care,
And fondly trod in each accustom'd path
That to the castle leads. Whilst thus I rang'd,
I was alarm'd with unexpected sounds
Of earnest voices. On the persons came:
Unseen I lurk'd, and overheard them name
Each other as they talk'd; Lord Randolph this,
And that Glenalvon: still of you they spoke,
And of the lady: threat'ning was their speech,
Though but imperfectly my ear could hear it.
'Twas strange, they said, a wonderful discov'ry;
And ever and anon they vow'd revenge.

DOUG. Revenge! For what?

O. NORV.   For being what you are,
Sir Malcolm's heir; How else have you offended?

When they were gone, I hied me to my cottage,
And there sat musing how I best might find
Means to inform you of their wicked purpose;
But I could think of none. At last, perplex'd,
I issued forth, encompassing the tower
With many a weary step and wishful look,
Now Providence hath brought you to my sight,
Let not your too courageous spirit scorn
The caution which I give.

  DOUG.   I scorn it not.
My mother warn'd me of Glenalvon's baseness:
But I will not suspect the noble Randolph.
In our encounter with the vile assassins
I mark'd his brave demeanor; him I'll trust.

  O. NORV. I fear you will, too far.

  DOUG.   Here in this place
I wait my mother's coming: she shall know
What thou hast told; her counsel I will follow:
And cautious ever are a mother's counsels.
You must depart; your presence may prevent
Our interview.

  O. NORV.   My blessing rest upon thee!
O may heav'n's hand, which sav'd thee from the wave
And from the sword of foes, be near thee still,
Turning mischance, if ought hangs o'er thy head,
All upon mine!   [*Exit.*

  DOUG.   He loves me like a parent;
And must not, shall not, lose the son he loves,
Although his son has found a nobler father.—
Eventful day, how hast thou chang'd my state!
Once on the cold and winter-shaded side
Of a bleak hill, mischance had rooted me,
Never to thrive, child of another soil.
Transplanted now to the gay sunny vale,
Like the green thorn of May my fortune flowers.

Ye glorious stars! high heav'n's resplendent host!
To whom I oft have of my lot complain'd,
Hear and record my soul's unalter'd wish!
Dead or alive, let me be but renown'd.
May heav'n inspire some fierce gigantic Dane
To give a bold defiance to our hoft!
Before he speaks it out, I will accept:
Like Douglas conquer! or, like Douglas die.
    Enter LADY RANDOLPH.
 LADY RAN. My son! I heard a voice—
 DOUG.   The voice was mine.
 LADY RAN. Didst thou complain aloud to Nature's
  ear,
That thus in dusky shades at midnight hours,
By stealth the mother and the son should meet.
         [Embracing him.
 DOUG. No: on this happy day, this better birth-day,
My thoughts and words are all of hope and joy.
 LADY RAN. Sad fear and melancholy still divide
The empire of my breast with hope and joy.
Now hear what I advise.
 DOUG.   First, let me tell
What may the tenor of your counsel change.
 LADY RAN. My heart forebodes some evil.
 DOUG.   'Tis not good—
At eve, unseen by Randolph and Glenalvon,
The good old Norval in the grove o'erheard
Their conversation: oft they mention'd me
With dreadful threat'nings; you they sometimes
  nam'd.
'Twas strange, they said, a wonderful discov'ry;
And ever and anon they vow'd revenge.
 LADY RAN. Defend us, gracious God! we are betray'd.
They have found out the secret of thy birth.
It must be so. That is the great discov'ry.

Sir Malcom's heir is come to claim his own;
And they will be reveng'd. Perhaps e'en now,
Arm'd and prepar'd for murder, they but wait
A darker and more silent hour, to break
Into the chamber where they think thou sleep'st.
This moment, this, heav'n hath ordain'd to save thee!
Fly to the camp, my son!

DOUG. And leave you here?
No: To the castle let us go together;
Call up the ancient servants of your house,
Who in their youth did eat your father's bread;
Then tell them loudly that I am your son.
If in the breasts of men one spark remains
Of sacred love, fidelity, or pity,
Some in your cause will arm. I ask but few
To drive those spoilers from my father's house.

LADY RAN. O nature, nature! what can check thy force?
Thou genuine offspring of the daring Douglas!
But rush not on destruction: save thyself,
And I am safe. To me they mean no harm.
Thy stay but risks thy precious life in vain.
That winding path conducts thee to the river.
Cross where thou seest a broad and beaten way,
Which, running eastward, leads thee to the camp.
Instant demand admittance to Lord Douglas.
Shew him these jewels which his brother wore.
Thy look, thy voice, will make him feel the truth,
Which I by certain proof will soon confirm.

DOUG. I yield me, and obey: But yet my heart
Bleeds at this parting. Something bids me stay
And guard a mother's life. Oft have I read
Of wond'rous deeds by one bold arm atchiev'd.
Our foes are two; no more; let me go forth,
And see if any shield can guard Glenalvon.

LADY RAN. If thou regárd'st thy mother, or rever'st
Thy father's mem'ry, think of this no more.
One thing I have to say before we part:
Long wert thou lost; and thou art found, my child,
In a most fearful season. War and battle
I have great cauſe to dread. Too well I see
Which way the current of thy temper sets.
To day I've found thee. Oh! my long lost hope!
If thou to giddy valour giv'st the rein,
To-morrow I may lose my son for ever.
The love of thee, before thou saw'st the light,
Sustain'd my life when thy brave father fell.
If thou shalt fall, I have nor love nor hope
In this waste world! My son, remember me!

DOUG. What shall I say? how can I give you comfort?
The God of battles of my life dispose
As may be best for you! for whose dear sake
I will not bear myself as I resolv'd.
But yet consider, as no vulgar name,
That which I boast, sounds amongst martial men,
How will inglorious caution suit my claim?
The post of fate unshrinking I maintain:
My country's foes must witness who I am.
On the invaders' heads I'll prove my birth,
Till friends and foes confess the genuine strain.
If in this strife I fall, blame not your son,
Who, if he lives not honour'd, must not live.

LADY RAN. I will not utter what my bosom feels.
Too well I love that valour which I warn.—
Farewell my son! my counsels are but vain; [*Embracing.*
And as high heav'n hath will'd it, all must be. [*Separate.*
Gaze not on me; thou wilt mistake the path;
I'll point it out again.

Just as they are separating, enter from the wood, RAN-
DOLPH *and* GLENALVON.

RAN. Not in her presence. Now———

GLEN. I'm prepar'd.

RAN. No: I command thee stay.
I go alone: it never shall be said
That I took odds to combat mortal man.
The noblest vengeance is the most complete.
[*Exit* Randolph.

[Glenalvon *makes some steps to the same side of the stage, listens, and speaks.*]

GLEN. Demons of death come settle on my sword,
And to a double slaughter guide it home!
The lover and the husband both must die.
[Randolph *behind the scenes.*

RAN. Draw, villain! draw.

DOUG. (*without*) Assail me not, Lord Randolph;
Not, as thou lov'st thyself. [*Clashing of swords.*
[Glenalvon *running out.*

GLEN. Now is the time.

Enter LADY RANDOLPH *at the opposite side of the stage, faint and breathless.*

LADY RAN. Lord Randolph, hear me; all shall be thine own:
But spare! O, spare my son!

Enter DOUGLAS *with a sword in each hand.*

DOUG. My mother's voice!
I can protect thee still.

LADY RAN. He lives, he lives:
For this, for this to Heav'n eternal praise!
But sure I saw thee fall.

DOUG. It was Glenalvon,
Just as my arm had master'd Randolph's sword,
The villain came behind me; but I slew him.

LADY RAN. Behind thee! Ah! thou'rt wounded:
O my child,
How pale thou look'st!—And shall I lose thee now?
DOUG. Do not despair: I feel a little faintness;
I hope it will not last. [*Leans upon his sword.*
LADY RAN. There is no hope!
And we must part! the hand of death is on thee!
O my beloved child! O Douglas! Douglas!
[Douglas *growing more and more faint.*
DOUG. Too soon we part: I have not long been
Douglas;
O destiny! hardly thou deal'st with me:
Clouded and hid, a stranger to myself,
In low and poor obscurity I liv'd.
LADY RAN. Has heav'n preserv'd thee for an end
like this!
DOUG. O, had I fall'n as my brave fathers fell,
Turning with great effort the tide of battle!
Like them I should have smil'd and welcom'd death.
But thus to perish by a villain's hand,
Cut off from nature's and from glory's course!
Which never mortal was so fond to run.
LADY RAN. Hear, Justice! hear! stretch thy avenging arm. [Douglas *falls.*
DOUG. Unknown I die. No tongue shall speak of
me.
Some noble spirits, judging by themselves,
May yet conjecture what I might have prov'd,
And think life only wanting to my fame.
But who shall comfort thee?
LADY RAN. Despair! despair!
DOUG. O, had it pleas'd high heav'n to let me live
A little while!———My eyes that gaze on thee
Grow dim apace!—My mother!—Oh! my mother!
[*Dies.*

Enter RANDOLPH *and* ANNA.

RAN. Thy words, the words of truth, have pierc'd
  my heart.
I am the stain of knighthood and of arms.
Oh! if my brave deliverer survives
The traitor's sword———— ———

ANN.   Alas! look there, my lord!
RAN. The mother and her son! How curst I am!
Was I the cause? No: I was not the cause.
Yon matchless villain did seduce my soul
To frantic jealousy.

ANN.   My lady lives:
The agony of grief hath but suppress'd
A while her powers.

RAN.   But my deliv'rer's dead!—
' The world did once esteem Lord Randolph well;
' Sincere of heart, for spotless honour fam'd:
' And in my early days, glory I gain'd
' Beneath the holy banner of the cross.
' Now past the noon of life, shame comes upon me;
' Reproach, and infamy, and public hate,
' Are near at hand; for all mankind will think
' That Randolph basely stabb'd Sir Malcolm's heir.'
            [Lady Randolph *recovering*.
LADY RAN. Where am I now? Still in this wretch-
  ed world!
Grief cannot break a heart so hard as mine.
' My youth was worn in anguish; but youth's strength,
' With hope's assistance, bore the brunt of sorrow;
' And train'd me on to be the object now,
' On which omnipotence displays itself,
' Making a spectacle, a tale of me,
' To awe its vassal, man.'

RAN.   O misery!————
Amidst thy raging grief I must proclaim

My innocence.
   LADY RAN.   Thy innocence!
   RAN.   My guilt
Is innocence compar'd with what thou think'st it.
   LADY RAN. Of thee I think not. What have I to do
With thee, or any thing?—My son! my son!
My beautiful! my brave! how proud was I
Of thee, and of thy valour! my fond heart
O'erflow'd this day with transport, when I thought
Of growing old amidst a race of thine,
Who might make up to me their father's childhood,
And bear my brother's and my husband's name:
Now all my hopes are dead!—A little while
Was I a wife! A mother not so long!
What am I now?——I know——But I shall be
That only whilst I please; for such a son
And such a husband make a woman bold. [*Runs out.*

   RAN. Follow her, Anna: I myself would follow;
But in this rage she must abhor my presence.
                        [*Exit* Anna.

          Enter OLD NORVAL.
   O. NORV. I heard the voice of woe: heav'n guard
     my child!
   RAN. Already is the idle gaping crowd,
The spiteful vulgar, come to gaze on Randolph.
Begone!
   O. NORV. I fear thee not. I will not go.
Here I'll remain. I'm an accomplice, lord!
With thee in murder. Yes; my sins did help
To crush down to the ground this lovely plant.—
O noblest youth that ever yet was born!
Sweetest and best, gentlest and bravest spirit
That ever blest the world!—Wretch that I am,
Who saw that noble spirit swell and rise
Above the narrow limits that confin'd it,

Yet never was by all thy virtues won
To do thee justice, and reveal the secret,
Which, timely known, had rais'd thee far above
The villain's snare. Oh! I am punish'd now!
These are the hairs that should have strew'd the ground,
And not the locks of Douglas.
[*Tears his hair, and throws himself upon the body of*
Douglas.

RAN. I know thee now: ' Thy boldness I forgive;
' My crest is fall'n.' For thee I will appoint
A place of rest, if grief will let thee rest.
I will reward, although I cannot punish.
Curst, curst Glenalvon; he escap'd too well,
Though slain and baffl'd by the hand he hated.
Foaming with rage and fury to the last,
Cursing his conqueror, the felon dy'd.

Enter ANNA.

ANN. My Lord! my Lord!
RAN.   Speak: I can hear of horror.
ANN. Horror, indeed!
RAN.   Matilda?——
ANN.   Is no more.
She ran, she flew like lightning up the hill,
Nor halted till the precipice she gain'd,
Beneath whose low'ring top the river falls
Ingulph'd in rifted rocks: thither she came,
As fearless as the eagle lights upon it,
And headlong down——— ———
RAN.   'Twas I! alas! 'twas I
That fill'd her breast with fury; drove her down
The precipice of death! Wretch that I am!
ANN. O had you seen her last despairing look!
Upon the brink she stood, and cast her eyes
Down on the deep: then lifting up her head
And her white hands to heav'n, seeming to say,

Why am I forc'd to this ? she plung'd herself
Into the empty air.

 RAN.   I will not vent,
In vain complaints, the passion of my soul.
Peace in this world I never can enjoy.
These wounds the gratitude of Randolph gave:
They speak aloud, and with the voice of fate
Denounce my doom. I am resolv'd. I'll go
Straight to the battle, where the man that makes
Me turn aside, must threaten worse than death.
Thou, faithful to thy mistress, take this ring,
Full warrant of my power. Let every rite
With cost and pomp upon her funerals wait;
For Randolph hopes he never shall return.
           [*Exeunt.*

THE END.

EPILOGUE.

AN Epilogue I ask'd; but not one word
Our bard will write. He vows 'tis most absurd
With comic wit to contradict the strain
Of Tragedy, and make your sorrows vain.
Sadly he says, that pity is the best,
The noblest passion of the human breast;
For when its sacred streams the heart o'erflow,
In gushes pleasure with the tide of woe;
And when its waves retire, like those of Nile,
They leave behind them such a golden soil,
That there the virtues without culture grow,
There the sweet blossoms of affection blow.
These were his words, void of delusive art;
I felt them; for he spoke them from his heart.
Nor will I now attempt, with witty folly,
To chace away celestial melancholy.

THE PADLOCK;

In Two Acts.

BY ISAAC BICKERSTAFF.

DRAMATIS PERSONAE.

	Drury-lane.	Edinburgh---1792.
MEN.		
DON DIEGO,	Mr. Bannister.	Mr. Baker.
LEANDER,	Mr. Vernon.	Mr. Bland *jun.*
MUNGO,	Mr. Dibdin.	Mr. Hallion.
WOMEN.		
LEONORA,	Mrs. Arne.	Miss Grist.
URSULA,	Mrs. Dorman.	Mrs. Charteris.

SCENE,---*A Garden belonging to* DON DIEGO'*s house.*

DON DIEGO *enters musing.*
AIR.

THOUGHTS to council——let me see—
Hum—to be or not to be
A husband, is the question.
A cuckold! must that follow?
Say what men will, wedlock's a pill
Bitter to swallow, and hard of digestion.
But fear makes the danger seem double.
Say, Hymen, what mischief can trouble
My peace should I venture to try you?
 My doors shall be lock'd, my windows be block'd;
 No male in my house, not so much as a mouse:
Then horns, horns, I defy you.

DIEG. Ursula!

Enter URSULA.

URS. Here, an't please your worship.

DIEG. Where is Leonora?

URS. In her chamber, Sir.

DIEG. There is the key of it; there the key of the best hall; there the key of the door upon the first flight of stairs; there the key of the door upon the second; this double-locks the hatch below, and this the door that opens into that entry.

URS. I am acquainted with every ward of them.

DIEG. You know, Ursula, when I took Leonora from her father and mother, she was to live in the house with me three months; at the expiration of which time, I entered into a bond of four thousand pistoles, either to return her to them spotless, with half that sum for her dowry, or make her my true and lawful wife.

URS. And I warrant you, they came secretly to inquire of me whether they might venture to trust your worship. Lord! said I, I have lived with the gentleman nine years and three quarters, come Lammas, and never saw any thing uncivil by him in my life: nor no more I ever did: and to let your worship know if I had, you would have mistaken your person; for I bless heaven, tho' I'm poor, I'm honest, and would not live with any man alive that should want to handle me unlawfully.

DIEG. Ursula, I do believe it: and you are particularly happy, that both your age and your person exempt you from any such temptation. But, be this as it will, Leonora's parents, after some little difficulty, consented to comply with my proposal; and, being fully satisfied with their daughter's temper and conduct, which I wanted to be acquainted with, this day being the expiration of the term, I am resolved to fulfil my bond, by marrying her to-morrow.

URS. Heaven bless you together.

DIEG. During the time she has lived with me, she has never been a moment out of my sight: and now tell me, Ursula, what you have observed in her.

URS. All meekness and gentleness, your worship; and yet, I warrant you, shrewd and sensible; egad, when she pleases, she can be as sharp as a needle.

DIEG. You have not been able to discover any particular attachment?

URS. Why, Sir, of late I have observed——

DIEG. Eh! how! what?

URS. That she has taken greatly to the young kitten.

DIEG. O! is that all?

URS. Aye, by my faith, I don't think she is fond of any thing else.

DIEG. Of me, Ursula?

URS. Ay, ay, of the kitten and your worship, and her birds, and going to mass. I have taken notice of late, that she is mighty fond of going to mass as your worship lets her, early of a morning.

DIEG. Well! I am now going to her parents, to let them know my resolution; I will not take her with me, because, having been used to confinement, and it being the life I am determined she shall lead, it will be only giving her a bad habit. I shall return with the good folks to-morrow morning; in the mean time, Ursula, I confide in your attention; and take care, as you would merit my favour.

URS. I will, indeed, your worship; nay, if there is a widow gentlewoman in all Salamanca fitter to look after a young maiden———

DIEG. Go, and send Leonora to me.

AIR.

URS. I know the world, Sir, tho' I say't:
   I'm cautious and wise;
   And they who surprise
   My prudence nodding, must sit up late,
   Never fear, Sir, your safety's here, Sir;
   Yes, yes, I'll answer for Miss:
     Let me alone,
   I warrant my care shall weigh to a hair
     As much as your own.   [*Exit* Ursula.

DIEG. I dreamt last night that I was going to church with Leonora to be married, and that we were met on the road by a drove of oxen.—— Oxen—I don't like oxen. I wish it had been a flock of sheep.

Enter LEONORA *with a bird on her finger, which she holds in the other hand by a string.*

LEO. Say, little foolish, fluttering thing,
    Whither, ah! whither would you wing
      Your airy flight?
Stay here and sing, your mistress to delight.
No, no, no,
Sweet Robin, you shall not go:
Where, you wanton, could you be
Half so hsppy as with me?

DIEG. Leonora!

LEO. Here I am.

DIEG. Look me in the face, and listen to me attentively.

LEO. There.

DIEG. I am going this evening to your father and mother, and I suppose you are not ignorant of the cause of my journey. Are you willing to be my wife?

LEO. I am willing to do whatever you and my father and mother please.

DIEG. But that's not the thing: do you like me?

LEO. Y—es.

DIEG. What do you sigh for?

LEO. I don't know.

DIEG. When you came hither, you were taken from a mean little house, ill situated, and worse furnished; you had no servants, and were obliged, with your mother, to do the work yourself.

LEO. Yes; but when we had done, I could look out at the window, or go a-walking in the fields.

DIEG. Perhaps you dislike confinement?

LEO. No, I don't, I'm sure.

DIEG. I say, then, I took you from that mean habitation and hard labour, to a noble building, and this fine garden; where, so far from being a slave, you are absolute mistress; and instead of wearing a mean stuff gown, look at yourself, I beseech you; the dress you have on is fit for a princess.

LEO. 'Tis very fine, indeed.

DIEG. Well, Leonora, you know in what manner you have been treated since you have been my companion; ask yourself again now, whether you can be content to lead a life with me according to the specimen you have had?

LEO. Specimen!

DIEG. Ay, according to the manner I have treated you——according——

LEO. I'll do whatever you please.

DIEG. Then, my dear, give me a kiss.

LEO. Good b'ye to you.

DIEG. Here, Ursula.

AIR.

By some I am told,
That I'm wrinkl'd and old;
  But I will not believe what they say:
I feel my blood mounting,
Like streams in a fountain,
  That merrily sparkle and play.
For love I have will,
And ability still;
  Odsbobs, I can scarcely refrain!
My diamond, my pearl——
Well, be a good girl,
  Until I come to you again. [*Exit* Diego.

LEO. Heigho!—I think I am sick.—He's very good to me, to be sure; and 'tis my duty to love him, because we ought not to be ungrateful; but I wish I was not to marry him for all that, though I'm afraid to tell him so. Fine feathers, they say, make fine birds; but I am sure they don't make happy ones; a sparrow is happier in the fields than a gold-finch in a cage. There is something makes me mighty uneasy. While he was talking to me, I thought I never saw any thing look so ugly in my life——— O dear now, why did I forget to ask leave to go to mass to-morrow? I suppose, because he's abroad, Ursula won't take me—I wish I had asked leave to go to mass.

AIR.

Was I a shepherd's maid to keep
On yonder plains a flock of sheep;
Well pleas'd I'd watch the live-long day,
My ewes at feed, my lambs at play.
Or would some bird that pity brings,
But for a moment lend its wings,
My parents then might rave and scold,
My guardians strive my will to hold:
Their words are harsh, his walls are high;
But spite of all, away I'd fly.

SCENE *changes to a street in Salamanca.* LEANDER *enters with two* Scholars; *all in their university gowns.*

LEAN. His name is Don Diego; there's his house, like another monastery, or rather prison; his servants are an ancient duenna, and a negro slave———

1*st* SCHO. And after having lived fifty years a bachelor, this old fellow has pick'd up a young thing of sixteen, whom he by chance saw in a balcony!

2*d.* SCHO. And you are in love with the girl?

LEA. To desperation; and I believe I am not indifferent to her; for finding that her jealous guardian took her to the chapel of a neighbouring convent every morning before it was light, I went there in the habit of a pilgrim, planting myself as near her as I could: I then varied my appearance; continuing to do so from time to time, till I was convinced she had sufficiently remarked and understood my meaning.

1*st* scho. Well, Leander, I'll say that for you, there is not a more industrious lad in the university of Salamanca, when a wench is to be ferreted.

2*d* scho. But prithee, tell us now, how did you get information?

LEAN. First from report, which raised my curiosity; and afterwards from the negro I just now mentioned: I observed that when the family was gone to bed, he often came to air himself at yonder grate; you know I am no bad chanter, nor a very scurvy minstrel; so taking a guitar, clapping a black patch on my eye, and a swathe upon one of my legs, I soon scraped acquaintance with my friend Mungo. He adores my songs and sarabands; and taking me for a poor cripple, often repays me with a share of his allowance; which I accept to avoid suspicion.

1*st* scho. And so———

LEAN. And so, Sir, he hath told me all the secrets of his family; and one worth knowing; for he informed me last night, that his master will this evening take a short journey into the country, from whence he proposes not to return till to-morrow, leaving his young wife, that is to be, behind him.

2*d* scho. Zounds! let's scale the wall.

LEAN. Fair and softly; I will this instant go and put on my disguise, watch for the Don's going out, attack my negro afresh, and try if by his means I cannot come into the house, or at least get a sight of my charming angel.

G 2

1st SCHO. Angel! is she then so handsome?

LEAN. It is time for us to withdraw: come to my chambers, and there you shall know all you can desire. [*Exit* Scholars.

AIR.

Hither, Venus, with your doves;
Hither, all ye little loves;
Round me light, your wings display,
And bear a lover on his way.
Oh, could I but, like Jove of old,
Transform myself to show'ry gold;
Or in a swan my passion shroud,
Or wrap it in an orient cloud,
What locks, what bars, should then impede,
Or keep me from my charming maid!

[*Exit* Leander.

SCENE *changes to the outside of* DON DIEGO'S *house, which appears with windows barr'd up, and an iron grate before an entry.* DON DIEGO *enters from the house, having first unlocked the door, and removed two or three bars which assisted in fastening it.*

DIEG. With the precautions I have taken, I think I run no risk in quitting my house for a short time; Leonora has never shown the least inclination to deceive me; besides, my old woman is prudent and faithful, she has all the keys, and will not part with them from herself. But suppose——suppose—— by the rood and St. Francis, I will not leave it in her power to do mischief—a woman's not having it in her power to deceive you is the best security for her fidelity, and the only one a wise man will confide in; Fast bind, safe find, is an excellent proverb. I'll e'en lock her up with the rest: there is a hasp to the door, and I have a padlock within which shall be my guarantee: I will wait till the negro returns with provisions he is gone to purchase; and clapping them all up together, make my mind easy by having the key they are under in my pocket.

Enter MUNGO *with a hamper.*

MUN. Go, get you down, you damn hamper, you carry me now. Curse my old Massa, sending me always here and dere for one something to make me tire like a mule—curse him imperance—and him damn insurance.

DIEG. How now?

MUN. Ah, Massa, bless your heart.

DIEG. What's that you are muttering, sirrah?

MUN. Noting, Massa; only me say, you very good Massa.

DIEG. What do you leave your load down there for?

MUN. Massa, me lily tire.

DIEG. Take it up, rascal.

MUN. Yes, bless your heart, Massa.

DIEG. No lay it down:—now I think on't, come hither.

MUN. What you say, Massa?

DIEG. Can you be honest?

MUN. Me no savee, Massa, you never ax me before?

DIEG. Can you tell truth?

MUN. What you give me, Massa?

DIEG. There's a pistern for you; now tell me, do you know of any ill going on in my house?

MUN. Ah, Massa, a damn deal.

DIEG. How, that I'm a stranger to?

MUN. No, Massa, you lick me every day with your rattan; I'm sure, Massa, that's mischief enough for poor Neger man.

DIEG. So, so.

MUN. La, Massa, how could you have a heart to

lick poor Neger man, as you lick me last Thursday?

DIEG. If you have not a mind I should chastise you now, hold your tongue.

MUN. Yes, Massa, if you no lick me again.

DIEG. Listen to me, I say.

MUN. You know, Massa, me very good servant—

DIEG. Then you will go on?

MUN. And ought to be use kine——

DIEG. If you utter another syllable———

MUN. And I'm sure, Massa, you can't deny but I worky worky—I dress a victuals, and run a errands, and wash a house, and make a beds, and scrub a shoes, and wait a table.

DIEG. Take that—Now will you listen to me?

MUN. La, Massa, if ever I saw———

DIEG. I am going abroad, and shall not return till to-morrow morning. During this night I charge you not to sleep a wink, but be watchful as a lynx, and keep walking up and down the entry, that if you hear the least noise, you may alarm the family.

MUN. So I must be stay in a cold all night, and have no sleep, and get no tanks neither; then him call me tief, and rogue, and rascal to tempt me.

DIEG. Stay here, perverse animal, and take care that nobody approaches the door; I am going in, and shall be out again in a moment.

AIR.

MUN. Dear heart, what a terrible life I am led!
A dog has a better, that's shelter'd and fed;
 Night and day 'tis de same,
 My pain is dere game:
Me wish to de Lord me was dead.
 Whate'ers to be done,
 Poor black must run:
 Mungo here, Mungo dere,
 Mungo every where;

Above and below,
Sirrah, come, sirrah, go;
Do so, and do so.
Oh, oh!
Me wish to de Lord me was dead.

[*Exit into the house.*

DON DIEGO *having entered the house during the song, returns with* URSULA, *who, after the Negro goes in, appears to bolt the door in the inside:* then DON DIEGO, *unseen by them, puts on a large padlock, and goes off. After which,* LEANDER *enters disguised, and* MUNGO *comes to the grate.*

LEA. So—my old Argus is departed, and the evening is as favourable for my design as I could wish. Now to attract my friend Mungo; if he is within hearing of my guitar, I am sure he will quickly make his appearance.

MUN. Who goes dere?—Hip, hollo!

LEA. Heaven bless you, my worthy master, will your worship's honour have a little music this evening? and I have got a bottle of delicious cordial here, given me by a charitable monk of a convent hard by, if your grace will please to taste it.

MUN. Give me a sup tro a grate; come closee man, don't be fear, old Massa gone out, as I say last night, and he no come back before to morrow; come, trike mousic, and give us a song.

LEA. I'll give your worship a song I learn'd in Barbary, when I was a slave among the Moors.

MUN. Ay, do.

LEA. There was a cruel and malicious Turk, who was called Heli Abdalah Mahomet Scah; now this wicked Turk had a fair Christian slave named Jezabel, who not consenting to his beastly desires, he draws out his sabre and is going to cut off her head;

here's what he says to her *(sings and plays)*. Now you shall hear the slave's answer *(sings and plays again)*. Now you shall hear how the wicked Turk, being greatly enraged, is again going to cut off the fair slave's head *(sings and plays again)*. Now you shall hear.———

MUN. What signify me hear?—Me no understand.

LEA. Oh, you want something you understand! If your honour had said that——

URSULA *above at the window.*

URS. Mungo! Mungo!

MUN. Some one call dere———

URS. Mungo, I say.

MUN. What devil you want?

URS. What lewd noise is that?

MUN. Lewd yourself; no lewd here; play away, never mind her.

URS. I shall come down if you go on.

MUN. Ay, come along, more merrier; nothing here but poor man, he sing for bit of bread.

URS. I'll have no poor man near our door: Hark'e, fellow, can you play the Forsaken Maid's Delight, or Black Bess of Castille? Ah, Mungo, if you had heard me sing when I was young!

MUN. Gad, I'm sure I hear your voice often enough now you old.

URS. I could quaver like any blackbird.

MUN. Come, throw a poor soul a penny, he play a tune for you.

URS. How did you lose the use of your leg?

LEA. In the wars, my good dame: I was taken by a Barbary corsair, and carried into Sallee, where I lived eleven years and three quarters upon cold water and the roots of the earth, without having a coat on my back, or laying my head on a pillow: an infidel bought me for a slave; he gave me the strappado on my shoulders, and the bastinado on the soles of my feet: now this infidel Turk had fifty-three wives, and one hundred and twelve concubines.

URS. Then he was an unreasonable villain.

LEONORA *above at the window.*

LEO. Ursula!

URS. Od's my life, what's here to do? Go back, go, back; fine work we shall have indeed; good man, good b'ye.

LEO. I could not stay any longer by myself; pray let me take a little air at the grate.

LEA. Do, worthy Madam, let the young gentlewoman stay, I'll play her a love-song for nothing.

URS. No, no, none of your love-songs here; if you could play a saraband indeed, and there was room for one's motion——

LEA. I am but a poor man, but if your ladyship will let me in as far as the hall or the kitchen, you may all dance, and I shan't ask any thing.

URS. Why, if it was not on my master's account, I should think no harm in a little innocent recreation.

MUN. Do, and let us dance.

LEO. Has Madam the keys then?

URS. Yes, yes, I have the keys.

LEA. Have you the key of this padlock too, Madam! Here's a padlock upon the door, heaven help us! large enough for a state-prison.

URS. Eh—how— what! a padlock?

MUN. Here it is, I feel it; adod, 'tis a tumper.

URS. He was afraid to trust me then!

MUN. And if the house was a-fire, we none of us get out to save ourselves.

LEA. Well, Madam, not to disappoint you and the young lady, I know the back of your garden-wall, and

I'll undertake to get up at the outside of it, if you can let me down on the other.

URS. Do you think you could with your lame leg?

LEA. O yes, Madam, I am very sure.

URS. Then, by my faith, you shall; for now I'm set on't.—A padlock! Mungo, come with me into the garden. [*Exit from the window.*

MUNGO *and* URSULA *going off,* LEANDER *and* LEONORA *are left together. The first part of the quintetto is sung by them in duet; then* MUNGO *and* URSULA *return one after another to the stations they had quitted.*

LEO. Pray, let me go with you.

LEA. Stay, charming creature: why will you fly the youth that adores you?

LEO. Oh, Lord! I'm frighted out of my wits!

LEA. Have you not taken notice, beauteous Leonora, of the pilgrim who has so often met you at church? I am that pilgrim, one who would change shapes as often as Proteus to be blessed with a sight of you.

  O thou whose charms enslave my heart,
  In pity hear a youth complain.

LEO. I must not hear—dear youth, depart—
  I'm certain I have no desert
  A gentleman like you to gain.

LEA. Then do I seek your love in vain?

LEO. It is another's right;

LEA.   And he,
  Distracting thought! must happy be,
  While I am doom'd to pain.

URS. Come round, young man, I've been to try.

MUN. And so have I.

A. 2. I'm sure the wall is not too high.
  If you please, you'll mount with ease.

LEA. Can you to aid my bliss deny?

Shall it be so?
If you say no, I will not go.
LEO. I must consent, however loath:
But, whenever we desire,
Make him promise to retire.
URS. Nay, marry, he shall take his oath.
LEA. By your eyes of heavenly blue;
By your lips ambrosial dew;
Your cheeks, where rose and lily blend;
Your voice, the music of the spheres—
MUN. Lord o'mercy how he swears!
He makes my hair all stand an end!
URS. Come, that's enough, ascend, ascend.
A. 4. Let's be happy while we may;
Now the old one's far away,
Laugh and sing, and dance and play;
Harmless pleasure, why delay?

ACT II.

Enter URSULA *and* LEANDER.

URS. Oh! shame; out upon't, Sir, talk to me no more; I that have been fam'd throughont all Spain, as I may say, for virtue and discretion; the very flower and quintessence of duennas; you have cast a blot upon me; a blot upon my reputation, that was as fair as a piece of white paper; and now I shall be reviled, pointed at; nay, men will call me filthy names on your account.

LEA. What filthy names will they call you?

URS. They'll say I'm an old procuress.

LEA. Fie, fie, men know better things—besides, tho' I have got admittance into your house, be assured I shall commit no outrage here; and if I have been guilty of any indiscretion, let love be my excuse.

URS. Well, as I live, he's a pretty young fellow.

LEA. You, my sweet Ursula, have known what it is to be in love; and, I warrant have had admirers often at your feet; your eyes still retain fire enough to tell me that.

URS. They tell you no lie; for, to be sure, when I was a young woman, I was greatly sought after; nay, it was reported that a youth died for love of me; one Joseph Perez, a tailor by trade; of the gre-hound make, lank; and, if my mem'ry fail me not, his right shoulder about the breadth of my hand higher than his left: but he was upright as an arrow; and, by all accounts, one of the finest workmen at a button-hole.

LEA. But where is Leonora?

URS. Where is she! by my troth, I have shut her up in her chamber, under three bolts and a double lock.

LEA. And will you not bring us together?

URS. Who I?—How can you ask me such a question? Really, Sir, I take it extremely unkind.

LEA. Well, but you misapprehend———

URS. I told you just now, that if you mentioned that to me again, it would make me sick; and so it has, turn'd me upside down as it were.

LEA. Indeed, my best friend———

URS. Oh, oh, hold me, or I shall fall.

LEA. I will hold you.

URS. And do you feel any compassion for me?

LEA. I do.

URS. Why, truly, you have a great deal to answer for, to bring tears into my eyes at this time o'day,

I'm sure they are the first I have shed since my poor dear husband's death.

LEA. Nay, don't think of that now.

URS. For you must understand, Sir, to play a trick upon a grave, discreet matron—And yet, after all, by my faith, I don't wonder you should love the young thing under my care; for it is one of the sweetest-conditioned souls that ever I was acquainted with; and, between ourselves, our Donee is too old for such a babe.

LEA. Ursula, take this gold.

URS. For what, Sir?

LEA. Only for the love of me.

URS. Nay, if that be all, I won't refuse it, for I love you, I assure you; you put me so much in mind of my poor dear husband; he was a handsome man; I remember he had a mole between his eye-brows, about the bigness of a hazel-nut; but, I must say, you have the advantage in the lower part of the countenance.

LEA. The old beldam grows amorous——

URS. Lord love you, you're a well-looking young man.

LEA. But Leonora——

URS. Ha, ha, ha! but to pretend you were lame— I never saw a finer leg in my life.

LEA. Leonora!

URS. Well, Sir, I'm going.

LEA. I shall never get rid of her.

URS. Sir——

LEA. How now?

URS. Would you be so kind, Sir, as to indulge me with the favour of a salute?

LEA. Ugh!

URS. Gad-a-mercy, your cheek—Well, well, I have

seen the day; but no matter, my wine's upon the lees now; however, Sir, you might have had the politeness when a gentlewoman made the offer.—But heaven bless you.

AIR.

'When a woman's front is wrinkled,
'And her hairs are sprinkled
'With grey, lack-a-day!
'How her lovers fall away!
'Like fashions past,
'Aside she's cast,
'No one respect will pay:
'Remember, lasses, remember,
'And while the sun shines make hay;
'You must not expect in December
'The flowers you gather'd in May.

[*Exit* Ursula.

Enter MUNGO.

MUN. Ah! Massa—You brave Massa, now, what you do here wid de old woman?

LEA. Where is your young mistress, Mungo?

MUN. By gog she lock her up. But why you no tell me before time you a gentleman?

LEA. Sure I have not given the purse for nothing.

MUN. Purse! what! you giving her money den?—curse her impurance, why you no give it me?—you give me something as well as she. You know, Massa, you see me first.

LEA. There, there, are you content?

MUN. Me get supper ready, and now me go to de cellar.—But I say, Massa, ax de old man now, what good him watching do, him bolts and him bars, him walls, and him padlock?

LEA. Hist! Leonora comes.

MUN. But, Massa, you say you teach me play.

AIR.

Let me, when my heart a-sinking,
Hear the sweet guitar a-clinking;
When a string speak,
Such moosic he make,
Me soon am cur'd of tinking.
Wid de toot, toot, toot,
Of a merry flute,
And cymbalo,
And tymbalo
To boot:
We dance and we sing,
Till we make a house ring,
And, tied in his garters, old Massa may swing.

[*Exit into the cellar.*

Enter LEONORA *and* URSULA.

LEA. Oh, charming Leonora, how shall I express the rapture of my heart upon this occasion? I almost doubt the kindness of that chance which has brought me thus happily to see, to speak to you, without restraint.

URS. Well, but it must not be without restraint; it can't be without restraint; it can't, by my faith; —now you are going to make me sick again.

LEO. La, Ursula, I durst to say the gentleman doesn't want to do me any harm.——Do you, Sir? I'm sure I would not hurt a hair of his head, nor nobody's else, for the lucre of the whole world.

URS. Come, Sir, where is your lute? You shall see me dance a saraband: or if you'd rather have a song ——or the child and I will move a minuet, if you choose grace before agility.

LEA. This fulsome harridan——

LEO. I don't know what's come over her, Sir! I never saw the like of her since I was born.

LEA. I wish she was at the devil.

LEO. Ursula, what's the matter with you?

URS. What's the matter with me! Marry come up, what's the matter with you? Signor Diego can't show such a shape as that; well, there is nothing I like better than to see a young fellow with a well-made leg.

LEA. Pr'ythee let us go away from her.

LEO. I don't know how to do it, Sir.

LEA. Nothing more easy; I will go with my guitar into the garden; 'tis moon-light, take an opportunity to follow me there: I swear to you, beautiful and innocent creature, you have nothing to apprehend.

LEO. No, Sir, I am certain of that, with a gentleman such as you are, and that have taken so much pains to come after me; and I should hold myself very ungrateful, if I did not do any thing to oblige you, in a civil way.

LEA. Then you'll come?

LEO. I'll do my best endeavour, Sir.

LEA. And may I hope that you love me?

LEO. I don't know; as to that I can't say.

URS. Come, come, what colloguing's here; I must see how things are going forward; besides, Sir, you ought to know that it is not manners to be getting into corners, and whispering before company.

LEA. Pshaw!

URS. Ay, you may say your pleasure, Sir; but I'm sure what I say is the right thing: I should hardly choose to venture in a corner with you myself; nay, I would not do it, I protest and vow.

LEA. Beautiful Leonora, I find my being depends upon the blessing of your good opinion; do you desire to put an end to my days?

Act II. THE PADLOCK. 23

LEO. No, indeed! Indeed I don't.
LEA. But then—

AIR.

In vain you bid your captive live,
  While you the means of life deny;
Give me your smiles, your wishes give
  To him who must without you die.
Shut from the sun's enliv'ning beam,
  Bid flow'rs retain their scent and hue;
Its source dry'd up, bid flow the stream,
  And me exist, depriv'd of you.

[*Exit* Leander.

URS. Let me sit down a little: come hither, child, I am going to give you good advice; therefore listen to me, for I have more years over my head than you.

LEO. Well, and what then?

URS. What then!—Marry, then you must mind what I say to you—as I said before—but I say—— what was I saying?

LEON. I'm sure I don't know.

URS. You see the young man that is gone out there; he has been telling me that he's dying for love of you; can you find in your heart to let him expire?

LEO. I'm sure I won't do any thing bad.

URS. Why, that's right; you learned that from me: have I not said to you a thousand times, Never do any thing bad? Have not I said it? answer me that.

LEA. Well, and what then?

URS. Very well, listen to me; your guardian is old, and ugly, and jealous, and yet he may live longer than a better man.

LEO. He has been very kind to me, for all that, Ursula, and I ought to strive to please him.

URS. There again; have I not said to you a thousand times, that he was very kind to you, and you

H 3.

ought to strive to please him? It would be a hard thing to be preaching from morning to night without any profit.

LEO. Well, Ursula, after all, I wish this gentleman had never got into the house; heaven send no ill come of it.

URS. Ay, I say so too; heaven send it; but I'm cruelly afraid; for how shall we get rid of him? he'll never be able to crawl up the inside of the wall, whatever he did the out.

LEO. O Lord! won't he?

URS. No, by my conscience, won't he; and when your guardian comes in, if we had fifty necks a-piece, he'd twist them every one, if he finds him here; for my part, the best I expect is to end my old days in a prison.

LEO. You don't say so?

URS. I do indeed, and it kills me to think of it; but every one has their evil day, and this has been mine.

LEO. I have promised to go to him into the garden.

URS. Nay, you may do any thing now, for we are undone; though I think, if you could persuade him to get up the chimney, and stay on the roof of the house until to-morrow night, we might then steal the keys from your guardian————but I'm afraid you won't be able to persuade him.

LEO. I'll go down upon my knees.

URS. Find him out, while I step up stairs.

LEO. Pray for us, dear Ursula.

URS. I will, if I possibly can.

AIR.

LEO. Oh me, oh me, what shall we do?
　　　The fault is all along of you:

You brought him in—why did you so?
'Twas not by my desire, you know.
We have but too much cause to fear
My guardian, when he comes to hear
We've had a man with us, will kill
Me, you, and all; indeed he will.
No penitence will pardon procure,
He'll kill us every soul, I'm sure. [*Exeunt.*

Enter DON DIEGO, *groping his way, with the padlock in his hand.*

DIEG. All dark, all quiet; gone to bed and fast asleep, I warrant them: however, I am not sorry that I altered my first intention of staying out the whole night; and meeting Leonora's father on the road was at any rate a lucky incident. I will not disturb them; but, since I have let myself in with my master key, go softly to bed; I shall be able to strike a light, and then I think I may say my cares are over. Good heavens!—what a dreadful deal of uneasinefs may mortals avoid by a little prudence! I doubt not now, there are some men who would have gone out in my situation, and, trusting to the goodness of fortune, left their house and their honour in the care of an inexperienced girl, or the discretion of a mercenary servant.—While he is abroad, he is tormented with fears and jealousies; and when he returns home, he probably finds disorder, and perhaps shame. But what do I do?——I put on a padlock on my door, and all is safe.

Enter MUNGO *from the cellar, with a flask in one hand, and a candle in the other.*

MUN. Tol, lol, lol, lol.
DIEG. Hold, didn't I hear a noise?
MUN. Hola.
DIEG. Heaven and earth! what do I see?

MUN. Where are you young Massa and Missy? Here wine for supper.

DIEG. I'm thunder-struck!

MUN. My old Massa little tink we be so merry—hic—hic—What's the matter with me? the room round.

DIEG. Wretch, do you know me?

MUN. Know you?——damn you.

DIEG. Horrid creature! what makes you here at this time of night? is it with a design to surprise the innocents in their beds, and murder them sleeping?

MUN. Hush, hush—make no noise—— hic—hic.

DIEG. The slave is intoxicated.

MUN. Make no noise, I say; deres young gentleman wid young lady; he play on guitar, and she like him better dan she like you. Fal, lal, lal.

DIEG. Monster, I'll make an example of you.

MUN. What you call me names for, you old dog?

DIEG. Does the villain dare to lift his hand against me?

MUNG. Will you fight?

DIEG. He's mad.

MUN. Deres one in the house you little tink. Gad he do you business.

DIEG. Go lie down in your stye, and sleep.

MUN. Sleep? sleep you self, you drunk——ha! ha! ha! Look, a padlock:—you put a padlock on a dore, again will you?—Ha, ha, ha!

DIEG. Didn't I hear music?

MUN. Hic—hic.

DIEG. Was it not the sound of a guitar?

MUN. Yes, he play on de guitar rarely——Give me hand; you're old rascal——an't you?

DIEG. What dreadful shock affects me! I'm in a

cold sweat; a mist comes over my eyes; and my knees knock together as if I had got a fit of the shaking palsy.

MUN. I tell you a word in your ear.

DIEG. Has any stranger broke into my house?

MUN. Yes, by——hic——a fine young gentleman, he now in next room with Missy.

DIEG. Holy Saint Francis! is it possible?

MUN. Go you round softly—you catch them together.

DIEG. Confusion! distraction! I shall run mad.

[*Exit* Mungo.

AIR.

Oh wherefore this terrible flurry?
My spirits are all in a hurry!
    And above and below,
    From my top to my toe,
Are running about hurry scurry.
My heart in my bosom a-bumping,
    Goes thumping,
    And jumping,
    And thumping:
Is't a spectre I see?
Hence vanish—Ah me!
    My senses deceive me;
    Soon reason will leave me:
What a wretch am I destined to be!

[*Exit* Don Diego.

Enter MUNGO, URSULA, LEANDER, *and* LEONORA.

URS. O shame! monstrous! you drunken swab, you have been in the cellar, with a plague to you.

MUN. Let me put my hands about you neck——

URS. Oh, I shall be ruin'd! Help, help! ruin, ruin!

LEO. Goodness me, what's the matter?

URS. O dear child, this black villain has frighten'd

me out of my wits; he has wanted———

MUN. Me, curse a heart, I want noting wid her—what she say I want for———

LEO. Ursula, the gentleman says he has some friends waiting for him at the other side of the garden-wall, that will throw him over a ladder made of ropes, which he got up by.

AIR.

LEA. Then must I go?

LEO. Yes, good Sir, yes.

LEA. A parting kiss?

LEO. No, good Sir, no.

LEA. It must be so.
 By this, and this,
 Here I could for ever grow.
 'Tis more than mortal bliss.

LEO. Well, now, good-night;
 Pray, ease our fright;
 You're very bold, Sir;
 Let loose your hold, Sir:
 I think you want to scare me quite.

LEAN. Oh fortune's spight!

LEO. Good night, good night.
 Hark! the neighb'ring convent's bell
 Tolls the vesper hour to tell;
 The cloak now chimes; a thousand times,
 A thousand times, farewell.

Enter DON DIEGO.

DIEG. Stay, Sir, let nobody go out of the room.

URS. *(falling down.)* Ah, ah! a ghost, a ghost!

DIEG. Woman, stand up.

URS. I won't, I wont: murder: don't touch me.

DIEG. Leonora, what am I to think of this?

LEO. Oh, dear Sir, don't kill me.

DIEG. Young man, who are you who have thus

clandestinely, at an unseasonable hour, broke into my house? Am I to consider you as a robber, or how?

LEAN. As one whom love has made indiscreet; of one whom love taught industry and art to compass his designs. I love the beautiful Leonora, and she me; but farther than what you hear and see, neither one nor the other have been culpable.

MUN. Hear him, hear him.

LEAN. Don Diego, you know my father well, Don Alphonso de Luna; I am a scholar of this university; and am willing to submit to whatever punishment he, thro' your means, shall inflict; but wreck not your vengeance here.

DIEG. Thus then my hopes and cares are at once frustrated; possessed of what I thought a jewel, I was desirous to keep it for myself; I raised up the walls of this house to a great height; I barr'd up my windows towards the street; I put double bolts on my doors; I banish'd all that had the shadow of man or male kind; and I stood continually centinel over it myself, to guard my suspicion from surprise: thus secur'd, I left my watch for one little moment, and in that moment——

LEO. Pray, pray, guardian, let me tell you the story, and you'll find I'm not to blame.

DIEG. No, child, I only am to blame, who should have considered that sixteen and sixty agree ill together. But tho' I was too old to be wise, I am not too old to learn; and so, I say, send for a smith directly, beat all the grates from my windows, take the locks from my doors, and let egress and regress be given freely.

LEO. And will you be my husband, Sir?

DIEG. No, child, I will give you to one that will

make you a better husband: here, young man, take
her: if your parents consent, to-morrow shall see you
join'd in the face of the church; and the dowry
which I promised her, in case of failure on my side
of the contract, shall now go with her as a marriage-
portion.

LEAN. Signor, this is so generous——

DIEG. No thanks; perhaps I owe acknowledge-
ments to you; but you, Ursula, have no excuse, no
passion to plead, and your age should have taught
you better. I'll give you five hundred crowns, but
never let me see you more.

MUNG. And what you give me, Massa?

DIEG. Bastinadoes for your drunkenness and infi-
delity. Call in my neighbours and friends. Oh!
man! man! how short is your foresight, how ineffectual your prudence, while the very means you use
are destructive of your ends!

AIR.

Go forge me fetters that shall bind
The rage of the tempestuous wind;
Sound with a needleful of thread
The depth of ocean's sleepy bed;
Snap like a twig the oak's tough tree,
Quench Etna with a cup of tea.
In these manoeuvres shew your skill,
Then hold a woman if you will.

URS. Permit me to put in a word.
My master here is quite absurd.
That men should rule our sex is meet;
But art, not force, must do the feat:
Remember what the fable says,
Where the sun's warm and melting rays
Soon bring about what wind and rain
With all their fuss attempt in vain.

Act II. THE PADLOCK. 31

MUN. And, Massa, be not angry, pray,
　　　If Neger man a word should say;
　　　Me have a fable pat as she,
　　　Which wid dis matter will agree.
　　'An owl once took it in his head
　　'Wid some young pretty bird to wed;
　　'But when his worship came to woo,'
　　　He could get none but de cuckoo.
LEO. Ye youth select, who wish to taste
　　　The joys of wedlock pure and chaste,
　　　Ne'er let the mistress and the friend
　　　An abject slave and tyrant end.
　　　While each with tender passion burns,
　　　Ascend the throne of rule by turns;
　　　And place (to love, to virtue juft)
　　　Security in mutual trust.
LEA. To sum up all you now have heard,
　　　Young men and old, peruse the bard:
　　'A female trusted to your care,'
　　　(His rule is pithy, short, and clear,)
　　'Be to her faults a little blind;
　　'Be to her virtues very kind;
　　'Let all her ways be unconfin'd;
　　'And clap your *padlock* on her mind.'

THE END.

I

SELECT MISCELLANIES

IN VERSE.

GIL MORRICE[*].

AN OLD SCOTTISH BALLAD.

Gil morrice was an erle's son
  His name it waxed wide;
It was nae for his great riches,
  Nor yit his meikle pride,
But for his dame, a lady gay
  Wha liv'd on Carron side.

'Whar sall I get a bonny boy
  'That will win hose and shoen,
'That will gae to lord Barnard's ha,
  'And bid his lady come?

'And ye maun rin errand Willie,
  'And ye maun rin wi speid;
'When ither boys gang on their feet,
  'Ye sall ha prancing steid.'

'O no! oh no! my master deir!
  'I dar na for my life;
'I'll no gae to the bauld baron's,
  'For to triest forth his wife.'

---

[*] From this ballad are taken the chief incidents of the Tragedy of Douglas.

' My bird Willie, my boy Willie,
  ' My deir Willie, he said,
' How can ye strive against the streim?
  ' For I sall be obey'd.'

' But O my master deir! he cryd,
  ' In grenewode ye're your lane :
' Gi owr sic thochts I wald ye red,
  ' For feir ye sold be tane.'

' Haste, haste, I say, gae to the ha,
  ' Bid her come here wi speid ;
' If ye refuse my hie command,
  ' I'll gar your body bleid.

' Gae bid her tak this gay mantel,
  ' Tis a gowd bot the hem ;
' Bid her come to the gude grenewode,
  ' Ein by hersel alane :

' And there it is, a silken sark,
  ' Her ain hand sew'd the sleive ;
' And bid her come to Gil Morrice ;
  ' Speir nae bauld baron's leive.'

' Yes I will gae your black errand,
  ' Thouch it be to your cost ;
' Sen ye will nae be warn'd by me,
  ' In it ye sall find frost.

' The baron he's a man o micht,
  ' He neir could bide to taunt :
' And ye will see before its nicht,
  ' Sma cause ye hae to vaunt.

' And sen I maun your errand rin,
  ' Sae sair against my will,
' I'se mak a vow, and keip it trow,
  ' It sall be done for ill.'

Whan he came to the broken brig,
   He bent his bow and swam ;
And whan he came to grass growing,
   Sat down his feet and ran.

And when he came to Barnard's yeat,
   Wold neither chap nor ca,
But set his bent bow to his breist,
   And lichtly lap the wa.

He wald na tell the man his errand
   Thoch he stude at the yeat ;
But straight into the ha he cam,
   Whar they were set at meat.

' Hail ! hail ! my gentle sire and dame !'
   ' My message winna wait,
' Dame, ye maun to the grenewode gae,
   ' Afore that it be late.

' Ye're bidden tak this gay mantel,
   ' Tis a gowd bot the hem :
' Ye maun haste to the gude grenewode,
   ' Ein by yoursel alane.

' And there it is, a silken sark,
   ' Your ain hand sewd the sleive ;
' Ye maun gae speik to Gil Morrice ;
   ' Speir nae bauld baron's leive.'

The lady stamped wi her foot,
   And winked wi her eie ;
But a that she cold say or do,
   Forbidden he wald nae be.

' It's surely to my bower-woman,
   ' It neir cold be to me.'
' I brocht it to lord Barnard's lady,
   ' I trow that ye be shee.'

Then up and spake the wylie nurse,
  (The bairn upon her knie,)
" If it be cum from Gil Morrice
  " It's deir welcum to me."

' Ye lie, ye lie, ye filthy nurse,
  ' Sae loud as I heir ye lie ;
' I brocht it to lord Barnard's lady,
  ' I trow ye be nae shee.'

Then up and spake the bauld baron,
  An angry man was he :
He has tane the table wi his foot,
  Sae has he wi his knie,
Till crystal cup and ezar dish
  In flinders he gard flie.

" Gae bring a robe of your cliding,
  " Wi a the haste ye can,
" And I'll gae to the gude grenewode,
  " And speak wi your leman."

' O bide at hame, now lord Barnard !
  ' I ward ye bide at hame ;
' Neir wyte a man for violence,
  ' Wha neir wyte ye wi nane.'

Gil Morrice sat in the grenewode,
  He whistled and he sang :
' O what meins a the folk coming ?
  ' My mother tarries lang.'

The baron to the grenewode cam,
  Wi meikle dule and care ;
And there he first spyd Gil Morrice,
  Kaming his yellow hair.

' Nae wonder, nae wonder, Gil Morrice,
  ' My lady loes thee weil.

' The fairest part of my body
  ' Is blacker than thy heil.

' Yet neir the less now, Gil Morrice,
  ' For a thy great bewtie,
' Ye'se rew the day ye eir was born;
  ' That head sall gae wi me.'

Now he has drawn his trusty brand,
  And slaided owr the strae;
And throuch Gil Morrice fair body
  He gar'd the cauld iron gae.

And he has tane Gil Morrice heid,
  And set it on a speir;
The meinest man in a his train,
  Has gotten that heid to beir.

And he has tane Gil Morrice up,
  Laid him across his steid;
And brocht him to his painted bower
  And laid him on a bed.

The lady on the castle wa
  Beheld baith dale and down;
And there she saw Gil Morrice heid
  Cum trailing to the toun.

' Better I loe that bluidy heid,
  ' Bot and that yellow hair,
' Than lord Barnard and a his lands
  ' As they lig here and there.'

And she has tane Gil Morrice heid,
  And kiss'd baith cheik and chin;
' I was anes fow of Gil Morrice
  ' As the hip is o the stane.

' I gat ye in my father's house
  ' Wi meikle sin and shame;

‘ I brocht ye up in the grenewode
  ‘ Ken'd to mysel alane :

‘ Aft have I by thy cradle sitten,
  ‘ And fondly sein thee sleip ;
‘ But now I maun gae 'bout thy grave
  ‘ A mother's teirs to weip.'

Again she kiss'd his bluidy cheik,
  Again his bluidy chin ;
‘ O better I looed my son Morrice,
  ‘ Than a' my kyth and kin !'

‘ Awa, awa, ye ill woman,
  ‘ An ill dethe may ye die !
‘ Gin I had ken'd he was your son
  ‘ He had neir been slayne by me.'

‘ Obraid me not, my lord Barnard !
  ‘ Obraid me not for shame !
‘ Wi that sam speir, O perce my heart,
  ‘ And save me frae my pain !

‘ Since naething but Gil Morrice heid
  ‘ Thy jealous rage cold quell,
‘ Let that same hand now tak her lyfe,
  ‘ That neir to thee did ill.

‘ To me nae after days nor nichts
  ‘ Will eir be saft or kind :
‘ I'll fill the air wi heavy sichs,
  ‘ And greit till I be blind.''

‘ Eneuch of bluid by me's been spilt,
  ‘ Seek not your dethe frae me ;
‘ I'd rather far it had been mysel,
  ‘ Than either him or thee.

‘ Wi hopeless wae I hear your plaint,
  ‘ Sair, sair, I rue the deid.—

'That eir this cursed hand of mine
  'Sold gar his body bleid!

'Dry up your teirs, my winsome dame,
  'They neir can heal the wound;
'Ye see his heid upon the speir,
  'His heart's bluid dyed the ground.

'I curse the hand that did the deid,
  'The heart that thought the ill
'The feet that bare me wi sic speid,
  'The comely youth to kill.

'I'll aye lament for Gil Morrice
  'As gin he war my ain;
'I'll neir forget the dreiry day
  'On which the youth was slain.'

ODE TO WOMEN.

BY MR. LOGAN.

YE virgins! fond to be admir'd,
With mighty rage of conquest fir'd,
  And universal sway;
Who heave th' uncover'd bosom high
And roll a fond, inviting eye,
  On all the circle gay!

You miss the fine and secret art
To win the castle of the heart,
  For which you all contend;
The coxcomb tribe may crowd your train,
But you will never, never gain
  A lover, or a friend.

If this your passion, this your praise,
Yo shine, to dazzle, and to blaze,
  You may be call'd divine:

But not a youth beneath the sky
Will say in secret, with a sigh
   ' O were that Maiden mine !'

You marshall, brilliant, from the box,
Fans, feathers, diamonds, castled looks,
   Your magazine of arms ;
But 'tis the sweet sequester'd walk,
The whisp'ring hour, the tender talk,
   That gives you genuine charms.

The nymph-like robe, the natural grace,
The smile, the native of the face
   Refinment without art ;
The eye where pure affection beams,
The tear from tenderness that streams,
   The accents of the heart ;

The trembling frame, the living cheek,
Where, like the morning, blushes break,
   To crimson o'er the breast ;
The look where sentiment is seen,
Fine passions moving o'er the mein,
   And all the soul exprest ;

Your beauties these ; with these you shine
And reign on high by right divine,
   The sov'reigns of the world :
Then to your court the nations flow,
The Muse with flow'rs the path will strew
   Where Venus' car is hurl'd.

From dazzling deluges of snow,
From summer noon's meridian glow,
   We turn our aking eye,
To Nature's robe of vernal green,
To the blue curtain all serene
   Of an Autumnal sky.

The fav'rite tree of beauty's Queen,
Behold the Myrtles modest green,
   The virgin of the grove!
Soft from the circlet of her star,
The tender turtles draw the car
   Of Venus and of Love.

The growing charm envites the eye:
See morning gradual paint the sky,
   With purple and with gold!
See spring approach with sweet delay!
See rose buds open to the ray,
   And leaf by leaf unfold!

We love th' alluring line of grace,
That leads the eye a wanton chace,
   And lets the fancy rove;
The walk of Beauty ever bends,
And still begins but never ends,
   The labyrinth of love.

At times, to veil, is to reveal,
And to display is to conceal,
   Mysterious are your laws!
The vision's finer than the view;
Her landscape nature never drew
   So fair as fancy draws.

A beauty, carelessly betray'd,
Enamours more, than if display'd
   All Woman's charms were giv'n;
And, o'er the bosom's vestal white,
The gauze appears a robe of light,
   That veils, yet opens, Heav'n.

See virgin Eve, with graces bland,
Fresh blooming from her maker's hands
   In orient beauty beam!

Fair on the river-margin laid,
She knew not that her image made
   The angel in the stream.

Still ancient Eden blooms your own,
But artless innocence alone
   Secures the heav'nly post;
For if beneath an angel's mein,
The serpent's tortuous train is seen,
   Our paradise is lost.

O nature, nature, thine the charm!
Thy colours woo, thy features warm,
   Thy accents win the heart!
Parisian paint of every kind,
That stains the body or the mind,
   Proclaims the harlot's art.

The midnight Minstrel of the grove
Who still renews the hymn of love
   And woos the wood to hear;
Knows not the sweetness of his strain,
Nor that above the tuneful train,
   He charms the lover's ear.

The zone of Venus, heav'nly-fine,
Is nature's handy-work divine,
   And not the web of att;
And they who wear it never know
To what enchanting charm they owe
   The empire of the heart.

SHIRREFS,
   PRINTER.

www.ingramcontent.com/pod-product-compliance
Lightning Source LLC
Chambersburg PA
CBHW021919180426
43199CB00032B/929